Forsake Him Not!

Knowing Who God Really Is

Curtis Welch

Treasure House

An Imprint of
Destiny Image
P.O. Box 310
Shippensburg, PA 17257

"For where your treasure is
there will your heart be also." Matthew 6:21

ISBN 1-56043-791-X

For Worldwide Distribution
Printed in the U.S.A.

Destiny Image books are available through these fine distributors outside the United States:

Christian Growth, Inc.
Jalan Kilang-Timor, Singapore 0315

Lifestream
Nottingham, England

Rhema Ministries Trading
Randburg, South Africa

Salvation Book Centre
Petaling, Jaya, Malaysia

Successful Christian Living
Capetown, Rep. of South Africa

Vision Resources
Ponsonby, Auckland, New Zealand

WA Buchanan Company
Geebung, Queensland, Australia

Word Alive
Niverville, Manitoba, Canada

Dedication

To my dear loving wife, Judy, who helped me type the manuscript and stood behind me as I compiled this book, and to my mother and children who encouraged me to complete it.

Endorsements

I doubt that I have read many books in which most segments are proven by the Word. Curt Welch's is a notable exception. If you read this book through, digesting the Word along with the text, I am convinced that your life will become more victorious. *Forsake Him Not!* should be on your "to read" list.

Edna Edwards, General Manager
Billy Graham Radio Station
WFGW/WMIT-FM

Curt Welch challenges us through God's Word to remember that the greatest desire of the believer should be to seek the presence of God in our worship, walk, work, and world. In our search for achievement, accomplishment, and recognition, let us *Forsake Him*

Not! This book needs to be read, and reread, by every pastor, seminary student and lay person.

Norm Sanders
The Billy Graham Training Center
at The Cove

Forsake Him Not! is simple reading with good examples and a solid foundation in the Scriptures. Curt Welch offers many practical helps that can easily be applied in our everyday walk.

Jerry Miller, Executive Director
The Billy Graham Training Center
at The Cove

How important it is to live as though God really does exist! Every believer will find *Forsake Him Not!* to be provocative, challenging, and inspirational.

John W. Minnema, Pastor
Hawthorne Gospel Church

Contents

Introduction

Forsake Him Not! is a book about drawing closer to God. It contains a portrait of my own life journey as I have walked with the Lord. The road has not been easy, but I am learning how to live victoriously. After 28 years, God has shown me through His Word how I can attain practical help for my life. He has made Himself real to me, and I know He can become real to you also.

Modern Christianity is not producing the kind of disciples the Bible teaches we should be. Many Christians do not truly know God. We have lost our understanding of who He is.

If we don't have a proper knowledge about God, we cannot know and experience His presence. Neither can we serve Him, because how can we walk with and serve a God we do not know. Similarly, worship loses its vitality when our understanding of God is deficient. Because we don't understand who He truly is, we see very little reason to thank and praise Him and we have no inclination to seek His comfort and security when the storms of life come our way.

This book is filled with Scriptures and practical ideas to help you understand better who God is and how you can live in an intimate relationship with Him. Pastors and counselors will find this book to be an excellent tool and resource, and leaders of discipleship training programs and Bible studies will want to consider it for use in their groups.

Chapter 1

Forsaking Him!

My people have committed two sins: They have forsaken Me, the spring of living water, and have dug their own cisterns, broken cisterns that cannot hold water (Jer. 2:13).

During the summer of 1988, we experienced a drought and were without water for many days. I had no alternative but to call a well driller. His schedule was so full that he could not come and measure for a well for at least two weeks. Meanwhile, our only sources of water were a river across the street and a spring eight miles away.

During this time, friends from New Jersey were visiting us. Our faith was running out, as we had previously experienced problems with the spring (the source of our drinking water), but the faith of our friend and her five-year-old son released a miracle. After our friend asked me where our spring was located, she and her son went down to it and prayed that we would have water again, and in greater abundance than we had enjoyed before.

The next morning, a Sunday, they left before dawn to return home. We used our bottled water to get ready for church, never thinking to check if the spring was yielding water. After we returned home, I decided to check the spring. To my amazement and God's glory, the holding tank was overflowing with water. From that day forward, that spring has supplied us with an abundance of water. We have also located two new springs!

In the midst of that drought, we failed to look to God and to trust Him to meet our needs. Instead, we tried to work out the problem through our own strength and abilities. We are not alone in this error. Many Christians try to live the Christian life by doing things according to their own plans and within their own power, leaving God entirely out of the picture.

The Misery of Forsaking God

Let us begin our study of how the believer can know the presence of God in his or her life by looking at the history of the nation of Israel and by applying their experiences to our lives. God promised the children of Israel that He would lead them out of Egypt into the promised land of Canaan. This journey from Egypt to Canaan is a portrait of the believer's walk into victory. Even as the Red Sea was a place of deliverance for the children of Israel, so the believer finds deliverance from the bondage of sin when he or she trusts Jesus as Savior and Lord.

The nation of Israel wandered in the wilderness for 40 years. Nearly all the first generation of wanderers never made it to the Promised Land because they failed to trust God. Only Joshua and Caleb, because they believed the promises of God, entered Canaan. Many Christians are no different from these Israelites. They persist in unbelief and ignorance, and suffer the resulting loss of the full and abundant life of victory God has promised and provided.

The difficult, wandering times of our lives are not brought to us to deprive us of God's blessings. Rather, God uses the testings and the trials of these so-called *wilderness periods* to make us grow stronger spiritually and to bring us closer to Him.

Unfortunately, some believers view these seasons of struggle as evidence of defeat in their Christian walks and, therefore, withdraw from God instead of seeking Him. In so doing, they forfeit the experience of living in God's presence and of receiving His blessings. This failure to live in relationship with God is evident in the second chapter of the Book of Jeremiah. As we consider how Israel failed God, let us examine ourselves to see how we have failed God in our Christian journey.

Let us examine our ways and test them, and let us return to the Lord (Lam. 3:40).

Forsaking God is refusing to acknowledge His deity and His loving-kindness. This leads to our failure to worship and praise Him.

As the Israelites journeyed to the Promised Land under God's leading, they began to put God aside and to act as though He had never existed. They went through their everyday lives pretending that God was not there and forgetting that He loved them and cared for them.

My people have committed two sins: **They have forsaken Me,** *the spring of living water...* (Jer. 2:13).

We as a nation today share this sin. We have forgotten who God really is.

Have *you* put God aside and neglected His presence in your daily life? Do you forget from time to time how great He is and how He truly cares for you in all that you do? Do worship and praise have little or no meaning for you? Beware lest you share the judgment suffered by the Israelites.

There is nothing more satisfying in life than having the security of knowing that God is with you. If you seek Him, you will find Him. Sadly, we often forfeit this security because our relationship with God is broken when we forsake Him. The Israelites felt God's judgment and were put to shame because they departed from the presence of God and rejected Him. We can expect the same sorrow when we forsake God.

O Lord, the hope of Israel, all who forsake You will be put to shame. Those who turn away from You will be written in the dust because they have forsaken the Lord, the spring of living water (Jer. 17:13).

The Lord always wants to be with you, but do you want to be with Him?

*The Lord is with you when you are with Him. If you seek Him, He will be found by you, **but if you forsake Him, He will forsake you** (2 Chron. 15:2b).*

Roadblocks to Spiritual Power

Psalms 106 and 107 show a more complete picture of Israel's failure in her relationship with God. As we look at these Scriptures, we will see both how Israel failed God and how we too put roadblocks between ourselves and God. These actions and attitudes, or roadblocks, always cause a loss of spiritual power.

1. Continuing to live in sin.

*We have sinned, even as our fathers did; we have **done wrong and acted wickedly** (Ps. 106:6).*

2. Living as though God doesn't exist.

*When our fathers were in Egypt, **they gave no thought to Your miracles;** they did not remember Your many kindnesses, and they rebelled by the sea, the Red Sea (Ps. 106:7).*

3. Forgetting the great things God has done and refusing His wisdom and His guidance in our lives.

But they soon forgot what He had done and did not wait for His counsel (Ps. 106:13).

4. Worshiping anything other than God.

At Horeb they made a calf and worshiped an idol cast from metal (Ps. 106:19).

5. Forgetting how God saved your soul.

They forgot the God who saved them, who had done great things in Egypt (Ps. 106:21).

6. Failing to trust God's Word.

Then they despised the pleasant land; they did not believe His promise (Ps. 106:24).

7. Complaining and grumbling before God.

They grumbled in their tents and *did not obey the Lord* (Ps. 106:25).

8. Doing evil, not good.

They provoked the Lord to anger by their wicked deeds, and a plague broke out among them (Ps. 106:29).

9. Refusing to allow the Holy Spirit to do His work in your life.

For they rebelled against the Spirit of God, and rash words came from Moses' lips (Ps. 106:33).

10. Neglecting to allow God's Word to advise and influence your Christian walk.

*For they had **rebelled against the words of God and despised the counsel of the Most High*** (Ps. 107:11).

11. Refusing to take the things of God seriously.

*Some became **fools through their rebellious ways and suffered affliction because of their iniquities*** (Ps. 107:17).

Limiting God

Psalm 78 provides a background of the history of Israel. The psalmist's purpose in writing this passage was to remind the people of his generation all the great things God had done in the past for His people. Let this be a lesson for us today.

Let us look together at Psalm 78:41, particularly the last part of the verse.

*Yea, they turned back and tempted God, and **limited the Holy One of Israel*** (Ps. 78:41 KJV).

Israel's purpose was to show forth God's power and might and to praise Him before the world. Instead, they were found to be disgraceful, complaining, rebellious, grumbling people who were continuously defeated by their enemies. They were guilty of "limiting God" (Ps. 78:41 KJV).

At this point, we need to examine ourselves against this text. Like Israel, believers are called to praise God before the world. The apostle Peter sets forth this mandate, which was first applied to Israel (see Deut. 7:6).

But you are a chosen people, a royal priesthood, a holy nation, a people belonging to God, that you may declare the praises of Him who called you out of darkness into His wonderful light (1 Pet. 2:9).

Many times, however, we are no different from the children of Israel. We limit God. Think about your own life. Do you understand and act on the truth that God called you out of this dark and sinful world to show forth His praises? Do you appreciate that God sent His Son Jesus into the world on *your* behalf? When was the last time you praised God for salvation?

Often we are not aware that we are limiting God. Perhaps the following list of the eight most common ways we limit God will help you to determine when and how you confine His work in your life.

1. Limiting God by our boundaries.

We limit God when we seek to live by His divine plan, working out what is good for us and changing our life styles for the better, only to set a boundary around our new lives and put God outside this border.

2. Failing to believe God's Word.

We limit God when we *say* that we believe the Bible is the definite Word of God but we do not *act* as though we believe all He says to us through the Scriptures. Whenever we allow situations and circumstances, for example, to shake our faith so that we fail to trust His word that He will supply all our needs, we limit His work for us.

3. Having an ungrateful attitude.

We limit God by our attitudes of ungratefulness, bitterness, complaining, and grumbling. When we are not thankful for what He has already done, we restrict what He yet can and will do in and through us.

4. Living in sin.

We limit God's showering of blessings into our lives by continuing in sin.

5. Saying no to God.

We short-circuit God's power in our lives when we resist His work in and through us. God's power does not change, but His use of it in our lives is bound by our refusal to obey Him and to cooperate with His word to us and His work in us.

6. Refusing to trust God's wisdom.

We limit God by failing to trust His perfect wisdom and to allow Him to be our guiding source throughout our daily lives.

7. Living from self-centeredness.

We limit God by letting self be the controlling factor in our lives. When God is not in the center of a believer's life, self-reliance replaces God in that person's world.

8. Viewing life through ignorance and blindness.

We limit God when we ignore and forget what He has done in the past and we become blind to what He is doing in the present. These shortcomings limit God's power in our lives.

We can blame no one but ourselves for these failures. Although God wants to lead us to Himself in the ways of holiness and righteousness, He will not force us to obey Him or to cooperate with His will.

Have you not brought this on yourselves by forsaking the Lord your God when He led you in the way? (Jer. 2:17)

If the presence and power of God are absent from your life, you are responsible. He wants to act with power for you and through you, but He works only for those who invite His actions. If you will not limit Him, He can and will do more than you can ever imagine.

Now to Him who is able to do immeasurably more than all we ask or imagine, according to His power that is at work within us (Eph. 3:20).

Satisfaction Within

My people have committed two sins: They have forsaken Me, the spring of living water... (Jer. 2:13).

Forsaking Jesus as the spring of living water is like depending on a river as your only source of water. When the river dries up, you have no water.

Jesus is your fountain of living water, a constant source of spiritual supply and blessings, *"for with* [Him] *is the fountain of life"* (Ps. 36:9a). You cannot live a godly life apart from Him because your spiritual life is empowered only when Jesus lives in your heart and His Spirit guides your soul. *"Christ in you, the hope of glory"* (Col. 1:27) is the secret to drawing from God's richness and wealth. This living presence of Jesus within begins when you accept Him as your Savior and Lord.

I have been crucified with Christ and I no longer live, but Christ lives in me. The life I live in the body, I live by faith in the Son of God, who loved me and gave Himself for me (Gal. 2:20).

Jesus used this image of *living water* to describe our spiritual life when we first believe in Him.

But whoever drinks the water I give him will never thirst. Indeed, the water I give him will become in him a spring of water welling up to eternal life (Jn. 4:14).

This living water comes into the life of a believer when he or she becomes born again (see Jn. 3:5). Jesus called this water *living water* because it is the life-giving source that not only keeps us alive but *makes* us alive. It does not merely refresh us but totally satisfies the deepest hungers of our hearts.

Physical water only reduces thirst temporarily, but the spiritual water from God quenches our inner thirst forever. It provides both divine power and eternal life. This water is a pure river flowing from the very presence of God (see Rev. 22:1).

Jesus promised us that His Spirit will live within us.

"Whoever believes in Me, as the Scripture has said, streams of living water will flow from within him." By this He meant the Spirit... (Jn. 7:38-39).

"From within him" refers to the manifestation of the Spirit in the life of the believer. When we believe on Jesus, rivers of living water flow from within us as the Holy Spirit controls our inner lives. Our old lives are like dried-up fountains, but our lives in Christ are filled with ever-flowing water because the source of our new fountain is found within the living God. As we remain in Christ, the water welling up within us can flow from us to meet the needs of other thirsty souls.

This spring of life-giving water will flow from within us not only in this life but throughout the life to come.

Never again will they hunger; never again will they thirst. The sun will not beat upon them, nor any scorching heat. For the Lamb at the center of the throne will be their shepherd; He will lead them to springs of living water (Rev. 7:16-17a).

Be careful, then, to let the Holy Spirit continually control your life, so that you are *"filled with the Spirit"* (Eph. 5:18).

Doing Things Our Way

*My people have committed two sins: They have forsake Me, the spring of living water, and **have dug their own cisterns, broken cisterns that cannot hold water** (Jer. 2:13).*

Cisterns were pits dug in the ground around a spring to retain water during the rainy season. Usually the pits were large, with a small opening at the top. This opening was closed with a large flat stone, which was then covered with sand. Eventually mud accumulated at the bottom of the pit. Thus, anyone who fell into these pits usually perished. Joseph was thrown into such a pit (Gen. 37:22), as was the prophet Jeremiah (Jer. 38:6).

This image of a cistern is a useful tool to help us understand the peril of relying on sources other than Jesus to meet our spiritual needs. Those who dig cisterns in the earth to retain rain water are often disappointed when they come to draw water for their needs. Because the pits have faulty bottoms that cannot hold water, they find only mud and other filthy sediments that can do nothing to quench their thirst.

So it is with those who refuse to go to Jesus for their spiritual fulfillment. Through their own strength they strive to meet their needs, but their digging proves to be unfruitful. In their hour of need, they find nothing to quench their thirst because their efforts are powerless to quench the spiritual thirst within.

Some Christian workers have learned the futility of seeking spiritual fulfillment from a source other than God. Having tried to serve God in their own strength and through their own efforts, they experience "spiritual burn-out," or in layman's terms, they become "stressed out."

The only power for deliverance from self-effort is found in Jesus. Only as we remain attached to Him can we truly serve God. (See chapter 15 of the Gospel of John.) He is the secret to satisfying the deep thirst of your heart and soul because the overflow of His Spirit within you is the only solution to the deep, spiritual thirst that is common to all people.

Changing Our Outlook

Now is the time to consider the importance of remaining faithful to Jesus and of letting Him be the Lord of our lives.

"Consider then and realize how evil and bitter it is for you when you forsake the Lord your God and have no awe of Me," declares the Lord, the Lord Almighty (Jer. 2:19b).

God will take us from the pit we have dug for ourselves, the pit of doing our own thing. The rock on which He places us is Jesus, our solid foundation of hope. Our position in Him will never be shaken.

He lifted me out of the slimy pit, out of the mud and mire; He set my feet on a rock and gave me a firm place to stand (Ps. 40:2).

True revival is realizing that we have drifted away from the Lord and wanting to return and bond our relationship with Him. Let us, then, with the children of Israel, resolve not to forsake Him. May the following verses be our prayer before God as we resist the temptation to forsake Him.

Then the people answered, "Far be it from us to forsake the Lord to serve other gods!" (Josh. 24:16)

Then we will not turn away from You; revive us, and we will call on Your name (Ps. 80:18).

There is going to be a day in your life when everything seems to fall apart and you can find nowhere to turn. The need to find a solution for your problem will be like the craving for water of a parched person. Apart from Jesus you will find no solution for that problem. He alone is the answer to your every need. He promises that He will never forget or abandon you.

*The poor and needy search for water, but there is none; their tongues are parched with thirst. But I the Lord will answer them; I, the God of Israel, **will not forsake them** (Is. 41:17).*

Jesus will be light to you in your darkest moments. Even when your problems seem to you as an unbearable heat, He will refresh you like a constant flowing stream of clear cool water, filling your soul with satisfaction and comforting you with His abiding presence within you.

*And if you spend yourselves in behalf of the hungry and satisfy the needs of the oppressed, then your light will rise in the darkness, and your night will become like the noonday. **The Lord will guide you always;** He will satisfy your needs in a sun-scorched land and will strengthen your frame. You will be like a well-watered garden, like a spring whose waters never fail (Is. 58:10-11).*

The Lord will never forget His faithful ones. No matter what harm or danger comes our way, He will always protect us, both in this life and the life to come.

*For the Lord loves the just and **will not forsake His faithful ones.** They will be protected forever... (Ps. 37:28).*

The writer of the Letter to the Hebrews, quoting from the Book of Deuteronomy, affirms this declaration of God's faithfulness.

*...God has said, "Never will I leave you; **never will I forsake you"** (Heb. 13:5).*

Jesus will never let you down. His faithfulness remains forever.

Chapter 2

Forsake Not His Presence!

Part 1

O God, You are my God, earnestly I seek You; my soul thirsts for You, my body longs for You, in a dry and weary land where there is no water. I have seen You in the sanctuary and beheld Your power and Your glory. Because Your love is better than life, my lips will glorify You. I will praise You as long as I live, and in Your name I will lift up my hands (Ps. 63:1-4).

This psalm was written by David after his son Absalom had turned against him, causing David to flee from Jerusalem into the wilderness. The physical wilderness or desert in which David found himself mirrored his condition—exiled from his home, his throne, and the sanctuary of his God. During that time of exile, David faced many difficulties and trials. Yet he never forsook God.

The secret to his perseverance is revealed in this psalm. Here David teaches saints from all ages how to handle the wearying, troublesome situations we all inevitably face. David consistently and trustingly relied on the goodness and the mercy of God.

We too must remember to rely on the goodness and the mercy of God, because every situation that comes our way is but a testing from God to determine the depth and constancy of our faith in Him. Too often when things are going "just great" in own eyes, we fall apart as soon as a crisis befalls us. We forget where to turn for help. Psalm 63 reveals David's prescription for such situations.

God Comes First

In spite of David's problems, he is careful to acknowledge God before turning to his own needs.

O God, You are my God... (Ps. 63:1).

Like David, we too must learn to put God first in our lives. When problems overtake us, we must reaffirm our relationship with Him and our need of Him before we enlist His aid. Reading the Bible, which is the Word of God, is a good place to begin because it turns our thoughts from ourselves to Him. Many of us are so caught up in our own little worlds, and our subjective understandings based upon our perceptions, that we have lost sight of our basic objective, which is to reveal God to the world.

Reading the Bible brings us back to God and encourages us to focus on His infinite majesty and power instead of our own finite thoughts and difficulties. The Scriptures also challenge us to declare our faith in the existence of God and to testify to His gracious actions on our behalf. As we focus on God through His Word and approach

Him through faith, we are then privileged to sense His presence, to walk with Him, and to please Him.

And without faith it is impossible to please God, because anyone who comes to Him must believe that He exists and that He rewards those who earnestly seek Him (Heb. 11:6).

This stance of faith permits us to move from the world in which we live, which is seen, to the realm of God's sovereignty, which is unseen, as "...*we fix our eyes not on what is seen, but on what is unseen. For what is seen is temporary, but what is unseen is eternal*" (2 Cor. 4:18).

Most of us have little trouble believing what we see every day with our physical eyes. Relying on the unseen world, which is spiritual and eternal, usually requires greater effort. We have trouble putting our faith in the invisible.

Consider the experience of a blind person. He must have faith both in the physical world that others see and in the spiritual world that is not visible to physical eyes. Those who work with blind people must help them to understand what goes on around them in the physical world and to trust in its existence. If for, example, a friend warns a blind person that he is approaching two steps, the blind individual must simply trust that there are two steps, not three.

In the same way, we must learn to accept what God says about the spiritual world that we cannot see. This takes faith in God and an understanding of the Scriptures. Both take time and effort.

Too often believers are so wrapped up in the everyday affairs of life that they seldom take the time or expend the effort to consider the invisible world. Pause a moment right now to consider the spiritual realm of faith. With the help of the Holy Spirit, exercise your eyes of faith to see the invisible world of God and to accept the reality of the presence of God and Jesus with you *now*. This unseen world of faith is the most important realm of your existence. You must recognize and explore this faith dimension every day.

Seeking God

O God, You are my God, earnestly I seek You... (Ps. 63:1).

The second thing David did was to make seeking God His first priority in the morning. In the original language, the word *earnestly* means "at dawn" or "in the morning." When you get up in the morning, do you seek God first before your busy day? Look to Jesus as your bright and morning star.

The Bible reveals only two things that God seeks: true worshipers— "...*true worshipers will worship the Father in spirit and in truth, for they are the kind of worshipers the Father seeks*" (Jn. 4:23)—and men who seek and understand Him—"*God looks down from heaven on the sons of men to see if there are any who understand, any who seek God*" (Ps. 53:2; see also Acts 17:27). God is pleased with us when we seek His presence. He desires that we should seek Him with all our hearts.

I love those who love Me, and those who seek Me find Me (Prov. 8:17).

You will seek Me and find Me when you seek Me with all your heart (Jer. 29:13).

Then let our reponse be,

My heart says of You, "Seek His face!" Your face, Lord, I will seek (Ps. 27:8).

Thirst for God

...my soul thirsts for You, my body longs for You, in a dry and weary land where there is no water (Ps. 63:1).

Third, David thirsted for God. His situation in the dry, waterless wilderness reminded him of the thirst of his soul for God. Because the Hebrew word for *soul* refers to one's whole being (as the *body*), this longing for God pertained to David's whole being.

Do you sometimes feel that your spiritual life is dull and dry as you journey through a barren desert? Does your soul cry out for something to quench its thirst for meaning and purpose? Are you seeking fulfillment in materialism, depending on other people for satisfaction, or trying to live a Christian life in your own strength and efforts? If your answer is yes, you are not alone.

Too often believers who have this thirst for meaning and purpose look in the wrong direction for fulfillment. The answers to your deepest longings cannot be found in the physical world. Only God can provide the complete satisfaction you seek. He is always ready to meet your every necessity at the precise moment of need. He understands your thirst and yearns to provide the means to quench your urgent desires, but He will not force you to accept His provisions.

David's soul longed for God like a thirsty deer searching for cool water after being chased by a hunter or a predator. So intense was his longing that his entire being cried out for God.

As the deer pants for streams of water, so my soul pants for You, O God (Ps. 42:1).

My soul yearns, even faints, for the courts of the Lord; my heart and my flesh cry out for the living God (Ps. 84:2).

Do you have a hunger and a thirst for God that consumes your entire being?

The Greatest Desire

O God, You are my God... Because Your love is better than life, my lips glorify You. ...My soul will be satisfied as with the richest of food (Ps. 63:1,3,5a).

The greatest desire of the believer should be to experience the presence of God. Most often God uses the thirst of your soul for meaning and fulfillment to create within you a desire for Himself. The Scriptures contain many examples of saints whose desire was to find and experience God's presence.

Moses desired to see God.

Then Moses said, "Now show me Your glory" (Ex. 33:18).

Job had the same goal.

If only I knew where to find Him; if only I could go to His dwelling! (Job 23:3)

David too longed to feel and sense the very presence of God.

Whom have I in heaven but You? And earth has nothing I desire besides You (Ps. 73:25).

David knew that nothing in Heaven or on earth can compare to God or satisfy like Him. Therefore, he desired above all else to gain God. (See also Philippians 3:7-8.) This desire flowed from previous encounters with the living God when he had experienced the richness of His presence.

Do you have the same burning desire to seek the face of God? Have you experienced the delight of His presence?

The House of God

I have seen You in the sanctuary and beheld Your power and Your glory (Ps. 63:2).

The Ark of the Covenant in the Tabernacle in Jerusalem was the symbol of the Lord's glory and strength. Many times David had worshiped in the Tabernacle and rejoiced in the presence of the living God. David yearned to experience in the wilderness the delights of

God he had known in God's sanctuary. David recalled with joy his participation there in worship.

These things I remember as I pour out my soul: how I used to go with the multitude, leading the procession to the house of God, with shouts of joy and thanksgiving among the festive throng (Ps. 42:4).

How lovely is Your dwelling place, O Lord Almighty! (Ps. 84:1)

I love the house where You live, O Lord, the place where Your glory dwells (Ps. 26:8).

One thing I ask of the Lord, this is what I seek: that I may dwell in the house of the Lord all the days of my life, to gaze upon the beauty of the Lord and to seek Him in His temple (Ps. 27:4).

David desired three things: to dwell in God's house, to behold the Lord, and to seek God's presence in His Temple. Yet David knew that God is not limited to a particular place. Therefore, he yearned to know in the wilderness the same presence of God he had experienced in the Tabernacle.

We too must learn this lesson. We can experience God's presence not only in our church buildings but in hospitals, prisons, and shelters for the homeless, and in our homes and our places of employment. Even in the wilderness, the times of testing in our lives, the presence of God is available to those who will seek it.

David found this to be true. Indeed, David found in his knowledge of God's loving-kindness the greatest comfort that was available to him. He had seen the power and glory of God in the sanctuary, therefore he could rejoice in God's loving-kindness in the wilderness. Hence, God's presence became more important to David than life itself.

> *Because Your love is better than life, my lips will glorify You. I will praise You as long as I live, and in Your name I will lift up my hands* (Ps. 63:3-4).

The physical hardships of David's wilderness experience and the pain of his separation from God's sanctuary did not change his desire to know and enjoy God's presence. The name of God and praise for God's loving-kindness continued to be on David's lips as he sought God and praised Him for His steadfast love. In the midst of his sojourn in the hot, dry desert, David was more concerned to find the refreshment of God's presence to sustain his spirit than the refreshment of cool water to sustain his body.

David's continual desire for God's presence is the secret to his victory over the disturbing thoughts that must have plagued his soul and spirit. As he placed his hope in God and focused on God's power by lifting up His name in praise, David turned his thoughts from his own problems to the majesty and the goodness of God.

> *Why are you downcast, O my soul? Why so disturbed within me? Put your hope in God, for I will yet praise Him, my Savior and my God. My soul is downcast within me; therefore I will remember You...* (Ps. 42:5-6).

David repeats this amazing affirmation of faith in God later in Psalm 42 (vs. 11) and again in Psalm 43 (vs. 5). He truly found victory because he sought God and relied on His power and mercy.

God wants us to discover this same victory. He cares so much for you and for me that He has preserved David's experiences in His Word so that we might learn from them. When life is difficult and you travel a rocky road or reach the end of your rope, what will you do? Will you look to God and praise Him for His goodness, or will you rely on your own strength and resources to pull you through? Will you continue to praise God, or will you grumble and complain because your situation or circumstances have disturbed your spirit?

I have found that looking to God and praising Him in the midst of difficult times raises my spirit and lifts me above my circumstances. You too can experience this victory. The crucial questions are, Do you value God's love over even your life? and, Do you praise Him in spite of your everyday circumstances? As you answer yes, you will find the refreshment in the wilderness that David experienced.

Knowing God

I have found Exodus 19:17 to be one of the most profound verses in the Old Testament.

Then Moses led the people out of the camp to meet with God, and they stood at the foot of the mountain (Ex. 19:17).

Before Moses would lead God's people to the Promised Land, they first had to meet with God.

The believer's journey of faith is no different. Before we can begin to worship God, to walk with Him, and to serve Him, we must first meet with Him. That is the goal of all worship services and the task of all who preach and lead in worship. These leaders are given the responsibility to escort God's people into His presence.

How different our worship services might be if we entered our church buildings *expecting* to be led to meet with God. Those who go to the house of God humbly and reverently, desiring and expecting to meet Him, will find Him. They will leave that place of worship saying, "Truly we have been brought into the glorious presence of Almighty God!"

Many churches today have a low view of God. Although they are very concerned to find better methods and more uplifting programs to increase the spiritual health of their people, the power of God is absent and their members are not experiencing spiritual growth. This is true because the congregation does not know and understand God. This failure to know and understand God will be disastrous for the Church because we cannot use God's power if we do not appreciate and delight in the Giver of that power.

What comes into your mind when you think about God? Do you see Him as an unchanging, holy, supreme, all-powerful, and majestic being, or do you tend to place Him on the same level as men and women? How would you describe Him? Have you met Him personally so that you truly know Him, or have you only heard about Him? If you reduce God to the level of human beings, you do not know the true living God, neither can you effectively worship Him. You cannot give honor to someone you do not know.

Today many people spend much time worrying about their physical bodies, their financial wealth, and their secular education. While health clubs, financial seminars, and colleges and technical schools are fine, if these become your priority, and you spend little time knowing and understanding God, you have missed the most important thing in life. The Scriptures are clear that knowing God is the foundation on which everything else rests.

*This is what the Lord says: "Let not the wise man boast of his wisdom or the strong man boast of his strength or the rich man boast of his riches, but let him who boasts boast about this: that he **understands** and **knows** Me, that I am the Lord, who exercises kindness, justice and righteousness on earth, for in these I delight," declares the Lord* (Jer. 9:23-24).

The Church must be committed to leading people to meet God. This occurs as we preach and study His Word and as we turn aside from the many preoccupations and obligations that deter us from spending the necessary time to discover the character and the nature of God. This knowledge must not be a casual acquaintance, for the word *know* pictures an intimate knowledge of God. God wants His people to be intimately acquainted with His kindness, justice, and righteousness.

Be still, and know that I am God (Ps. 46:10a).

This intimate knowing cannot be a one-time learning, but a day-by-day experience of studying His Word and learning more about Him.

Let us acknowledge the Lord; let us press on to acknowledge Him (Hos. 6:3a).

Can you properly define *eternal life*? Most people respond that eternal life is "time without end" or they say that eternal life keeps Christians from experiencing eternal hell. Yes, these things are true, but the Bible gives us a fuller, more definite answer concerning the nature of eternal life.

The gospel of God is more than knowing about Jesus and having eternal life. The good news of God in Christ is that we may know **God** intimately through His Son Jesus. This is the purpose of eternal life.

Now this is eternal life: that they may know You, the only true God, and Jesus Christ, whom You have sent (Jn. 17:3).

Thus, the true definition of eternal life is knowing God and Jesus. The apostle Paul knew the supreme value of this knowledge. His burning desire was that he and others would seek and grow in the knowledge of God.

What is more, I consider everything a loss compared to the surpassing greatness of knowing Christ Jesus my Lord, for whose sake I have lost all things. I consider them rubbish, that I may gain Christ (Phil. 3:8).

For this reason, since the day we heard about you, we have not stopped praying for you and asking God to fill you with the knowledge of His will through all spiritual wisdom and understanding. And we pray this in order that you may live a life worthy of the Lord and may please Him in every way: bearing fruit in every good work, growing in the knowledge of God (Col. 1:9-10).

The apostle Peter shared Paul's concern.

But grow in the grace and knowledge of our Lord and Savior Jesus Christ (2 Pet. 3:18a).

Nothing in this world, with all its wealth and materialism, can match the joy and wonder of knowing Jesus. Knowing God through Jesus Christ is the key to spiritual growth and maturity. Make this increase in the knowledge and understanding of God your personal goal. Read your Bible daily and ask God to teach you about Himself. Take the apostle Paul's prayer for the Ephesians and make it your own, "...*asking that the God of our Lord Jesus Christ, the glorious Father, may give you the Spirit of wisdom and revelation, so that you may know Him better*" (Eph. 1:17). Then may you know that the Lord is God, and that He is turning your heart back to Himself (see 1 Kings 18:37).

Knowing God's Character

As you study the Scriptures, you will discover some of the characteristics of God that reveal who He really is. For example, the Old and New Testaments reveal the following aspects of God's nature:

- Self-existent (Ps. 36:9)
- Eternal (Rev. 1:8)

- Unchanging (Heb. 13:8)
- Omnipresent (Jer. 23:23)
- Wise (Jer. 10:12)
- Holy (Ex. 15:11)
- All-Knowing (Ps. 139:1-6)
- All-Powerful (Rev. 19:1)
- Righteous (1 Cor. 1:30)
- Faithful (Ps. 33:4)
- Good (2 Chron. 7:3)
- Loving (Rom. 8:38-39)
- Merciful (Neh. 9:31)
- Patient (1 Tim. 1:16)
- Gracious (Tit. 3:5-7)
- Supreme (Col. 1:15-19)
- Sovereign (Is. 46:10)
- The One and Only God (Deut. 6:4)
- Majestic (Jude 25).

Knowing God's Name

Secondly, we can learn more about God by knowing His various names. This knowledge can both give us a better understanding of Him and help us through life's difficulties because God's names reveal Him to us in a more personal way.

*Those who **know Your name** will trust in You, for You, Lord, have never forsaken those who seek You (Ps. 9:10).*

Some trust in chariots and some in horses, but we trust in the name of the Lord our God (Ps. 20:7).

"Because he loves Me," says the Lord, "I will rescue him; I will protect him, for he acknowledges My name" (Ps. 91:14)

Not to us, O Lord, not to us but to Your name be the glory, because of Your love and faithfulness (Ps. 115:1).

I will bow down toward Your holy temple and will praise Your name for Your love and Your faithfulness, for You have exalted above all things Your name and Your word (Ps. 138:2).

Knowing the different names of God and Jesus also strengthens our faith and enables us to trust God more because we know how to acknowledge Him. Take, for example, the knowledge that God is a *strong tower.*

The name of the Lord is a strong tower; the righteous run to it and are safe (Prov. 18:10).

When a believer knows God by this name, he can run to God for protection in the midst of trouble. Had he not known this name of God, this individual may not have expected God to protect him from harm and danger.

This is not a unique example. Knowing God's names can help us to trust God and acknowledge His power in a variety of situations. Perhaps you are facing a financial crisis. Then your prayer might include the name *Jehovah-Jireh* (the Lord will provide [Gen 22:14]) in the following manner: "Oh, Lord, You are my provider, and I trust that You will meet my financial needs today." Or again, you may be facing difficulties that are beyond your strength. Then you might pray using the name *Jehovah Tsuri* (O Lord, my strength [Ps. 19:14 (KJV); Rock (NIV)]): "Oh, Lord, You are my strength, and I ask You to help me during my surgery."

Knowing the various names of God will give power to your Christian life if you use them in a personal way. Then you can address God from the perspective of your knowledge that He has the resources to meet your specific needs. Prayer using the names of God helps us to move from abstract reliance on God to dependence in a specific situation.

The Benefits of Knowing God

Taking time to know God has many benefits for our personal lives.

- We receive grace and peace (2 Pet. 1:2).
- We see God's glory (Hab. 2:14).
- We can rely on God's love for us (1 Jn. 4:16).
- We receive the knowledge of salvation through the forgiveness of our sins (Lk. 1:77).
- We can recognize and appreciate God's truth (1 Tim. 2:3-4).
- We are privileged to use God's spiritual wisdom and understanding to learn His will for His people (Col. 1:9).
- We recognize God's Son, Jesus Christ, and share in His sufferings and power (Phil. 3:10).
- We come to understand God's Word to us through the Scriptures (Acts 18:24).
- We see and understand the secrets of God's Kingdom (Lk. 8:10).
- We receive the Holy Spirit, who reveals the truth of God (Jn. 16:13-14).
- We enjoy the security of God's protection (Ps. 91:14).
- We grow into spiritual maturity as we are transformed into the fullness of Christ (Eph. 4:13).

Chapter 3

Forsake Not His Presence!

Part 2

Look to the Lord and His strength; seek His face always (Ps. 105:4).

Admission Into God's Presence

Do you ever feel that God is far away? When you pray, do you fear that God doesn't hear you? By what authority do you enter His presence?

The Word of God verifies that every believer has the privilege of entering into the very presence of God. Many Christians, however, do not fully accept this right because they do not understand their standing and position in Jesus Christ. Therefore, they fearfully seek the Lord and they doubt His presence and work in their lives. If this is your experience, it is imperative that you pay close attention to the truths contained in this chapter.

The blood of Jesus gives the believer the power and the boldness to enter the Most Holy Place, the very dwelling place of God. In the Old Testament, the Most Holy Place was in the center of the Tabernacle and the Temple. This meeting place between God and His people was available only to the High Priest, and to him only once a year. Once a year, on the Day of Atonement, he entered this sacred area to sprinkle the blood of a goat and a bull on the altar to atone for the sins of God's people. Through the priest, the children of Israel met God there.

Since the atoning death of Jesus Christ, God's people have direct access to this meeting place. We no longer need a human priest to meet with God on our behalf because Jesus is our priest. The shedding of His blood has opened the way for us to meet directly with God.

Therefore, brothers, since we have confidence to enter the Most Holy Place by the blood of Jesus...and since we have a great priest over the house of God, let us draw near to God with a sincere heart in full assurance of faith... (Heb. 10:19,21-22).

But now in Christ Jesus you who once were far away have been brought near through the blood of Christ (Eph. 2:13).

This privilege to enter God's presence is based not on our performance or efforts, but on our faith in Jesus and His atoning sacrifice on our behalf. He is both the means for our perfect standing before God and the provision for our direct access to the Father. His merit permits us to approach our heavenly Father with freedom and confidence because His righteousness becomes our righteousness (see 1 Cor. 1:30).

Therefore, since we have been justified through faith, we have peace with God through our Lord Jesus Christ, through whom we have gained access by faith into this grace in which we now stand. And we rejoice in the hope of the glory of God (Rom. 5:1-2).

This access to the presence of God is available to us at all times through God's indwelling Spirit within us. As the Holy Spirit filled the Most Holy Place behind the veil, so the Spirit fills our souls, *"for through Him* [Jesus Christ] *we…have access to the Father by one Spirit"* (Eph. 2:18). We must be careful, however, not to quench the Holy Spirit because then we can no longer feel and sense His presence within us. Then we lose the fellowship of God's presence.

Therefore, *"let us draw near to God with a sincere heart in full assurance of faith…"* (Heb. 10:22). Paul is speaking here not to certain individuals, but to all who are in the faith. This closeness with God is a gift for all who receive Jesus Christ as Savior, not only for a privileged few. God wants His people to experience the closeness of His abiding presence, and He offers that opportunity to all who come to Him through the sacrificial death of Jesus Christ. Whether you accept His gift and use the opportunity He offers is your choice.

The Presence of God

God is eternal, although eternity is greater than man's understanding. He is also everywhere at all times, not being confined to any particular place. In essence, He has no limits upon His existence.

This presence of God, which is at the same time evident in my life and yours, can be compared to the presence of the sun. Although the sun is millions of miles away from the earth, through the brightness of its rays it is present in the lives of all touched by its light and warmth. So it is with the presence of God. No matter where you are on earth, or indeed throughout this universe and the galaxies beyond,

God is present there. He knows intimately all that goes on throughout His creation and He governs both the world we know and the unseen worlds beyond our experience. We can, thus, be sure that He knows us perfectly and understands the totality of our lives.

"Can anyone hide in secret places so that I cannot see him?" declares the Lord. "Do not I fill heaven and earth?" declares the Lord (Jer. 23:24).

God...is not far from each one of us. "For in Him we live and move and have our being" (Acts 17:27-28a).

Where can I go from Your Spirit? Where can I flee from Your presence? If I go up to the heavens, You are there; if I make my bed in the depths, You are there. If I rise on the wings of the dawn, if I settle on the far side of the sea, even there Your hand will guide me, Your right hand will hold me fast. If I say, "Surely the darkness will hide me and the light become night around me," even the darkness will not be dark to You; the night will shine like the day, for darkness is as light to You (Ps. 139:7-12).

This should be a comforting thought for believers, knowing that wherever we are, we can have the peace and the security of knowing that God is with us and He oversees everything that goes on in our lives.

God's presence can best be understood as we envision His holiness and majesty. When we approach His throne through the eyes of faith, we see that He is radiant with glory.

Who among the gods is like You, O Lord? Who is like You—majestic in holiness, awesome in glory, working wonders? (Ex. 15:11)

Picture God in your mind's eye as a great king enthroned above the universe. Always He is attended and served by an innumerable host of heavenly beings who carry out His every command. His holiness fills the throne room.

...Therefore hear the word of the Lord: I saw the Lord sitting on His throne with all the host of heaven standing around Him on His right and on His left (1 Kings 22:19; see also Ps. 96:7; 104:1-4; Dan. 7:9-10).

...I saw the Lord seated on a throne, high and exalted, and the train of His robe filled the temple. Above Him were seraphs, each with six wings: With two wings they covered their faces, with two they covered their feet, and with two they were flying. And they were calling to one another: "Holy, holy, holy is the Lord Almighty; the whole earth is full of His glory" (Is. 6:1-3).

Then picture Jesus, enthroned in glory at the right hand of God with creatures and elders bowing before Him in worship and adoration.

In a loud voice they sang: "Worthy is the Lamb, who was slain, to receive power and wealth and wisdom and strength and honor and glory and praise!" Then I heard every creature in heaven and on earth and under the earth and on the sea, and all that is in them, singing, "To Him who sits on the throne and to the Lamb be praise and honor and glory and power, for ever and ever!" The four living creatures said, "Amen," and the elders fell down and worshiped (Rev. 5:12-14).

This majesty, glory, and holiness of God should make us approach His presence with great humility. Yet we often belittle the awesome reality of God with our casual use of today's much-used phrase, "This is awesome." This inconsiderate use belittles the God who truly is awesome.

You are awesome, O God, in Your sanctuary; the God of Israel gives power and strength to His people. Praise be to God! (Ps. 68:35)

Finally, let's picture the throne of God as standing on the twin pillars of righteousness and perfect judgment, with pure, perfect love and absolute faithfulness informing both.

Righteousness and justice are the foundation of Your throne; love and faithfulness go before You (Ps. 89:14).

This displays God's true character.

Awareness of God's Presence

When we are aware of God's presence, He becomes real to us. As I was preparing this book, I shared the first chapter with a friend. As we were talking about it, the presence of God surrounded us so that both of us felt it.

Every believer must learn to exercise and cultivate this awareness of God's presence. At first this may feel awkward—something like driving a car or playing an instrument for the first time—but in time this consciousness of the presence and anointing of God will become an integral part of your life.

Pause right now and be still. Think about God and His presence in and around you. This may seem strange, but if you persevere, God will manifest Himself to you. Then you will experience one of the greatest moments of your journey of faith. You will meet the awesome, holy God.

If our churches would teach believers how to discover and enjoy the presence of God, our lives would never be the same. Meeting a living God gives life to dry faith. This was the experience of Jacob, who met God in a place he did not expect Him.

When Jacob awoke from his sleep, he thought, "Surely the Lord is in this place, and I was not aware of it." He was afraid and said, "How awesome is this place! This is none other than the house of God; this is the gate of heaven "(Gen. 28:16-17).

This awareness of God's presence occurs as we are still before Him (Ps. 46:10) and as we learn to sense His nearness. Many Christians find the discipline of seeking God with silent expectation to be very difficult. This is true because our world focuses on busyness and noise instead of solitude and silence. When we fail to take time to reflect on the greatness of God, we are apt to make excuses for our failure. In truth, this neglecting of fellowship and conversation with God is sin. Any time something takes the time or the honor that belong to God alone, we have made that thing an idol. Then when trials come our way, we fail to walk in victory and wonder why God does not work on our behalf.

Very often God does not work for us because we have neither sought His presence nor walked through our daily lives with an awareness of His activity in and through us. Sadly, only a small percentage of believers have this awareness of God's presence in their lives.

When the prophet Isaiah experienced this new awareness of God's presence, he became conscious of his need for cleansing.

...I saw the Lord seated on a throne, high and exalted, and the train of His robe filled the temple. Above Him were seraphs...and they were calling to one another: "Holy, holy, holy is the Lord Almighty; the whole earth is full of His glory." At the sound of their voices the doorposts and thresholds shook and the temple was filled with smoke. "Woe is me!" I cried. "I am ruined! For I am a man of unclean

lips...and my eyes have seen the King, the Lord Almighty" (Is. 6:1-5).

How does a believer develop this awareness of God? Begin first by reading and praying God's Word. As you read the Scriptures, God will speak to you. Then pray back to God what you have just read. Next, come quietly and humbly to the Lord. Be still and calm as you begin to sense His presence with you. Look within yourself where God dwells (see 1 Cor. 3:16; 6:19). As you develop your awareness of God's presence, you will grow in spiritual maturity. In time you will sense His presence throughout your life—at work and at home, on solitary walks and in the company of other people.

How would you act if God visibly appeared to you when you were alone? Would you approach Him with reverence and a serious attitude, or would you bow your head in shame because you were not aware of His presence until He manifested Himself before you?

The answer to this question has important implications because you cannot be serious about your Christian life and remain oblivious to God's presence. The more you cultivate your awareness of Him, the more you will sense His company. When you are distracted during prayer and worship, try to sense His presence. As you seek to resist temptations, actively call Him to mind. Then you will be surprised and delighted as the presence and the power of God enlighten and empower you. Then you will truly meet the Most Holy One.

Set God Before You

If we could ask King David to share with us his favorite verse from the Book of Psalms, I believe he would recite the following words:

I have set the Lord always before me. Because He is at my right hand, I will not be shaken (Ps. 16:8).

This thought was the secret to David's victorious life. He continually set the Lord before him by consciously placing himself in God's presence. You, too, can develop this approach to life. As you consciously seek God's presence, you will become aware that He has been with you all the time. This seeking is not a passive action. Rather you must determine to put God first in all parts of your life and to act on His Word as He sets it before you.

Knowing what God requires but failing to do it cannot help you to mature in Him. Rather you must knowingly make Him the first and last thoughts of your day. Only as you come to Him for guidance and act on what He shows you will His presence become meaningful and precious. Even as a hiker must use a compass to determine the direction he should go, so you must seek the wisdom and knowledge of God to direct your steps.

God is the indicator that marks your path to victory. Until you focus on Him with awareness and set your life before Him with deliberate listening and obedience, you cannot hope to walk in His paths and to fulfill His purposes. David's motto, "I have set the Lord before me always," is the key to a victorious Christian life. As you begin your day by setting yourself before the Lord so that He is always before you, you will learn to sense His presence and to walk in His ways.

Chapter 4

Forsake Him Not in Worship!

Part 1

Ascribe to the Lord the glory due His name; worship the Lord in the splendor of His holiness (Ps. 29:2).

As we begin to experience the presence of God, we should be drawn to worship Him. What is worship? Is it important for us to worship God? How do we become worshipers?

For us to rightly worship God, we must first have a proper knowledge and understanding of Him, because our worship can be no greater than our knowledge of Him. If you have a low view and understanding of God, worship will have little or no impact on your Christian life. The more you know about God, the greater your response to Him in worship will be.

Sing ye praises with understanding (Ps. 47:7b KJV).

I know that the Lord is great, that our Lord is greater than all gods (Ps. 135:5).

The eleventh chapter of the Book of Hebrews, by the arrangement of the verses, shows the proper order for our Christians lives. First, we need to have faith in God.

Now faith is being sure of what we hope for and certain of what we do not see. …without faith it is impossible to please God, because anyone who comes to Him must believe that He exists and that He rewards those who earnestly seek Him (Heb. 11:1,6).

Worshiping God shows faith on the part of the believer.

Second, we must worship God. Abel's sacrifice is a picture of *worship.*

By faith Abel offered God a better sacrifice than Cain did (Heb. 11:4a).

Third, we must walk with God. Enoch demonstrates this necessary step in our Christian lives.

By faith Enoch was taken from this life, so that he did not experience death; he could not be found, because God had taken him away. For before he was taken, he was commended as one who pleased God (Heb. 11:5).

Enoch walked with God; then he was no more, because God took him away (Gen. 5:24).

Finally, we must be obedient in service to God. Noah exemplified this aspect of our Christian journey when he built the ark at God's command.

By faith Noah, when warned about things not yet seen, in holy fear built an ark to save his family (Heb. 11:7a).

Some believers emphasize service to God over worship. Others stress the priority of worship. We must be careful not to hold up one truth of the Bible to the exclusion or the diminishing of another. This is not scriptural. Rather we must view and apply the truths of God from a balanced perspective. Thus, we see that Jesus said, "...*it is written: 'Worship the Lord your God, and serve Him only' "* (Mt. 4:10). This divine order for the Christian life—worship, walk, serve— is the basis for the sequence of this chapter and the two chapters that follow it.

The Meaning of Worship

The Hebrew word for worship (*sachan*) means in the Old Testament "to bow oneself down, crouch, fall down (flat), humbly beseech, do (make) obeisance, and to do reverence." In the New Testament, the Greek word for worship (*proskuneo*) means "to kiss (like a dog licking his master's hand); to fawn or crouch; to (literally or figuratively) prostrate oneself in homage (do reverence to, adore). "

For example, we have a dog that comes up to us and kisses our hands every time we come home or go outside. This is an expression of his complete love and respect for us and his loyalty to us. I can always count on my dog, whether day or night, to greet me by licking my hand.

How much love, loyalty, and respect do you show for God? Worship demands that we enter God's presence, because it brings us face to face with God and His Son in a spirit of awe and reverential fear. Although we can bow at God's feet in worship (see Gen. 24:48), to kiss His hand is to show a more intimate closeness with Him. This closeness is God's highest desire for His relationship with His children.

The Background of Worship

Worship, a theme that runs throughout the Bible, is first mentioned in the Book of Genesis:

[Abraham] *said to his servants, "Stay here with the donkey while I and the boy go over there. We will worship and then we will come back to you"* (Gen. 22:5).

The Scriptures abundantly reveal that worship is a response not to church activity and programs, but to the Almighty God and the Lord Jesus Christ. God Himself must be our primary purpose for going to church on Sunday. For this reason, Sunday morning at church has been known as the "morning worship hour."

Although all churches make worship part of their religious activities, many see worship as a noun rather than a verb. The planned program is emphasized instead of the activity of the believers as they lift their spirits to God. Worship must never become a spectator experience, because a verb requires action.

True worship does not require fancy buildings, big pipe organs, stained-glass windows, robed choirs, or a minister behind a pulpit. These may prepare us for worship, but they must not become a substitute for worship. While planned activities and a preplanned order for worship services can be beneficial to *lead* us into worship, they can never *be* worship. Whether in private or in the midst of the community of faith, true worship moves believers beyond the planned program to active communication between man and God.

Worship in the Old Testament

The Old Testament contains many instructions concerning worship, both to govern it and to impress upon the people the importance God attaches to it. First, the Law commanded God's people to worship only Him.

You shall have no other gods before Me. You shall not make for yourself an idol.... . You shall not bow down to them or worship them; for I, the Lord your God, am a jealous God... (Ex. 20:3-5).

Do not worship any other god, for the Lord, whose name is Jealous, is a jealous God (Ex. 34:14).

Second, the Old Testament commands the Israelites to assemble together before God at various feasts. There they were to acknowledge and worship Him according to His instructions.

But you are to seek the place the Lord your God will choose from among all your tribes to put His Name there for His dwelling. To that place you must go (Deut. 12:5).

Shiloh was the first place God selected for His people to gather in worship. The Tabernacle was built there before it was taken to Jerusalem.

Year after year this man went up from his town to worship and sacrifice to the Lord Almighty at Shiloh... (1 Sam. 1:3).

Third, the Old Testament's description of the building of the Tabernacle reveals God's concern for worship. The purpose of the Tabernacle was to give God a dwelling place among His people so they could meet with Him. The Ark of the Covenant was the place within the Tabernacle where God chose to dwell. This was the first piece of furniture God described to Moses.

There, above the cover between the two cherubim that are over the ark of the Testimony, I will meet with you and give you all My commands for the Israelites (Ex. 25:22).

Fourth, the Old Testament reveals the importance of worship in its recording of the specific instructions given by God for the building of the Temple and for the prescribed worship there. Like its predecessor, the Tabernacle, the Temple was constructed to give God a home among His people where they could worship Him. Detailed instructions covered every aspect of that worship.

Stand at the gate of the Lord's house and there proclaim this message: "Hear the word of the Lord, all you people of Judah who come through these gates to worship the Lord" (Jer. 7:2).

Deliver to the God of Jerusalem all the articles entrusted to you for worship in the temple of your God (Ezra 7:19).

The prince is to enter from the outside through the portico of the gateway and stand by the gatepost. The priests are to sacrifice his burnt offering and his fellowship offerings. He is to worship at the threshold of the gateway and then go out, but the gate will not be shut until evening (Ezek. 46:2).

When the people of the land come before the Lord at the appointed feasts, whoever enters by the north gate to worship is to go out the south gate; and whoever enters by the south gate is to go out the north gate. No one is to return through the gate by which he entered, but each is to go out the opposite gate (Ezek. 46:9).

God Commands Us to Worship Him

Come, let us bow down in worship, let us kneel before the Lord our Maker (Ps. 95:6).

God invites us to come and worship Him. This invitation, however, does not mean that worship is optional. Notice that *come*, the first word in this verse, is a word of calling or command that in the Hebrew means "to go in, enter, or come." Worship is commanded by God for His people.

We worship God because we belong to Him. He is our Creator who guards us like a shepherd watches over and cares for his sheep.

"...for He is our God and we are the people of His pasture, the flock under His care" (Ps. 95:7a).

God expects us to come before Him in reverence, submission, and holiness. A deep awe before His divine majesty, power, and glory is to be our attitude in His holy presence. (See Psalm 5:7, Second Kings 17:36, and Revelation 14:7 and 15:4.)

Worship the Lord in the splendor of His holiness; tremble before Him, all the earth (Ps. 96:9).

Worshiping God is the most glorious deed the believer can do. Any believer who goes into the very presence of God to worship Him will never be the same when he leaves God's presence. Only as we present our lives and will before God can we begin to see our lives transformed by Jesus. This process of renewal will lead us to a life of holiness (see Lev. 19:2). Holiness begins as we present ourselves before God in worship.

Therefore, I urge you, brothers, in view of God's mercy, to offer your bodies as living sacrifices, holy and pleasing to God—this is your spiritual act of worship (Rom. 12:1).

Exalt the Lord our God and worship at His footstool; He is holy (Ps. 99:5).

The primary reason we worship the Lord is because He is holy. His holiness is evident as soon as we enter His presence. This is what should compel us to bow before Him with reverence and awe, for His holiness beams upon worshipers like the rays of the sun. The prophet Isaiah, for example, was prompted to worship the Lord when he saw God on His throne and he heard the living creatures that surrounded Him calling out one to another, *"Holy, holy, holy is the Lord Almighty*" (Is. 6:3). An awareness of God's holiness was the basis for his worship.

We Worship God

In the early stages of biblical history, God commanded His people not to worship or serve other gods. Thus, He constantly reminded the Israelites that He, the true living God who had led them out of Egypt, is the only God worthy of their praise and adoration. Not only were they not to worship other gods, they were not to bow down to or worship any other thing because this places an idol before the Lord.

> *When the Lord made a covenant with the Israelites, He commanded them: "Do not worship any other gods or bow down to them, serve them or sacrifice to them. But the Lord, who brought you up out of Egypt with mighty power and outstretched arm, is the one you must worship. To Him you shall bow down and to Him offer sacrifices* (2 Kings 17:35-36).

The Lord alone is the Creator of this vast universe. When my wife and I go out at night and see the many stars and planets, we cannot comprehend how God made them. We stand in awe before such a great God. Too often God's people take His marvelous gifts for granted, including life itself, and forget to worship Him for all the wonders He has created. The multitudes in Heaven worship and praise God for His creative genius. We should join them in worship.

> *You alone are the Lord. You made the heavens, even the highest heavens, and all their starry host, the earth and all that is on it, the seas and all that is in them. You give life to everything, and the multitudes of heaven worship You* (Neh. 9:6).

God does not want His people to worship false images and idols made by man. This worship of anything other than God is sin in His eyes. Yet, we easily succumb to the temptation to place something before God in our lives.

Is there anything in your life—a loved one, a friend, your career, material possessions, your own self—that you put before God? If you were to stand before the Lord right now, would you feel shame because other people and things have become your gods and not the Lord Himself? Please take this matter of worshiping God seriously. If you do not, someday you will look back and realize that you have sinned by failing to enthrone the Lord as the God of your life. Then, shame will fill you.

All who worship images are put to shame, those who boast in idols—worship Him, all you gods! (Ps. 97:7)

Christ Is Central to Worship

In the Gospel of Matthew, the first book of the New Testament, we read that magi came to worship Jesus when He was born. They knew that He was the Son of God.

On coming to the house, they saw the child with His mother Mary, and they bowed down and worshiped Him. Then they opened their treasures and presented Him with gifts of gold and of incense and of myrrh (Mt. 2:11).

The disciples, having witnessed the power of Jesus over creation, also worshiped Him.

Then those who were in the boat worshiped Him, saying, "Truly You are the Son of God" (Mt. 14:33).

Mary Magdalene and the other Mary also worshiped the Lord when, with joy, fear, and excitement, they saw the resurrected Savior.

Suddenly Jesus met them. "Greetings," He said. They came to Him, clasped His feet and worshiped Him (Mt. 28:9).

The revelation of John also shows us that Jesus, who is central in the Scriptures, is to be the center of our worship. On two occasions when John fell down to worship the one who was leading him in his vision, the angel forbade him to worship him, saying, *"I am a fellow servant with your brothers who hold to the testimony of Jesus. Worship God!"* (Rev. 19:10b; see also Rev. 22:8)

This awareness that Jesus Christ is the Son of God must also be central to our worship. The next time you read one of the Gospels, meditate on Jesus' words and let them become life for you. Then present yourself before Christ in worship. One day all creation will join in that worship, giving Jesus Christ the honor that is His due.

Therefore God exalted Him to the highest place and gave Him the name that is above every name, that at the name of Jesus every knee should bow, in heaven and on earth and under the earth, and every tongue confess that Jesus Christ is Lord, to the glory of God the Father (Phil. 2:9-11).

And again, when God brings His firstborn into the world, He says, "Let all God's angels worship Him" (Heb. 1:6).

Those in God's Presence Worship Him

The purpose of the Bible is to show us the One who is the object of our worship. True worship is being in the presence of God. The Book of Revelation, in particular, shows the nature of true worship.

All the angels were standing around the throne and around the elders and the four living creatures. They fell down on their faces before the throne and worshiped God (Rev. 7:11).

And the twenty-four elders, who were seated on their thrones before God, fell on their faces and worshiped God (Rev. 11:16).

Who will not fear You, O Lord, and bring glory to Your name? For You alone are holy. All nations will come and worship before You, for Your righteous acts have been revealed (Rev. 15:4; see also Rev. 4:10; 5:14; 19:4).

The question has been asked, "What will we do in Heaven?" This I know for certain. We will join all the heavenly hosts in worshiping God and Jesus throughout eternity. We will not worship God's Kingdom, but God Himself.

Therefore, since we are receiving a kingdom that cannot be shaken, let us be thankful, and so worship God acceptably with reverence and awe, for our "God is a consuming fire" (Heb. 12:28-29).

This eternal worship must begin in our life on earth. If you worship God on Sunday morning, do you worship Him on Monday? If not, you must evaluate whether you are truly worshiping Him. Resolve now to create within yourself a hunger and a desire to worship God that does not wait for Sunday morning but enters His presence throughout the week. God desires that you should continually live in His presence, bringing Him the worship that belongs only to Him.

Let us go to His dwelling place; let us worship at His footstool (Ps. 132:7).

God Seeks Worshipers

Jesus is the most-qualified teacher on the subject of worship. In His conversation with the Samaritan woman at the well, He showed her a new meaning of worship. When she questioned Him concerning the right place for worship—*"Our fathers worshiped on this mountain, but you Jews claim that the place where we must worship is in Jerusalem* (Jn. 4:20)—Jesus replied that worship need not be confined to a particular place or a certain building— "Believe Me, *woman, a time is coming when you will worship the Father neither on this mountain nor in Jerusalem* (Jn. 4:21b). This must have astonished the woman because the Old Testament clearly states that the Tabernacle and the Temple were God's dwelling place among His people. They were designed by God for the sole purpose of providing a place where God's people could worship Him.

Since the coming of Jesus, these buildings are no longer needed as *the* place of worship because they were but a shadow or a picture of the true temple, which is Jesus. (See Hebrews 9:22-28.) Through His atoning death, Jesus opened the way for us to enter into the Most Holy Place of God's presence. This place of worship is no longer confined to a particular place, but has now become a spiritual state. All who accept Jesus as their Savior and Lord now have the freedom to worship God without having to go to a certain building to meet Him. You can worship God in any part of your house or out of doors. You can worship while you work or play. This is true because the essential ingredient for worship is not a place, but the desires and the condition of your heart. If Jesus lives in your heart, you are now a temple in which God dwells (1 Cor. 3:16-17).

Yet a time is coming and has now come when the true worshipers will worship the Father in spirit and in truth, for they are the kind of worshipers the Father seeks (Jn. 4:23).

Jesus is pointing here to His Father as the object of our worship. Worship that is *"in spirit and in truth"* must be spiritual, not of the flesh, and it must be centered in truth. Truth consists of three things. First, Jesus is truth (Jn. 14:6); second, the Word of God is truth (Eph. 1:13); and third, the Holy Spirit is truth (Jn. 16:13). The Holy Spirit teaches and guides the believer from the Word of God, which reveals Jesus. Thus, two things are needed for us to effectively worship God: the Scriptures and the Holy Spirit. Without these, we will worship in the flesh.

This spiritual worship is the purpose for our existence. The Father *seeks* worshipers. It is evident, then, that our response to God's call to worship Him cannot be a casual response. Unfortunately, God finds very few who worship Him in spirit and in truth. Are you a true worshiper of God?

Prayer, the Pathway to Worship
There is a wealth of information available on the subject of prayer. My purpose here is to help you see how prayer relates to worship.

1. Prayer brings you into God's presence.

In the last chapter, we discussed briefly how to come into God's presence by *setting the Lord before us.* Now, I want you to see something very interesting.

I have set the Lord always before me (Ps. 16:8a).

May my prayer be set before You like incense; may the lifting up of my hands be like the evening sacrifice (Ps. 141:2).

Setting the Lord before us brings us into His presence. Setting our prayers before the Lord does the same thing. Incense, here, is a picture of worship as our prayers ascend to God as a pleasant aroma. Worship, thus, involves coming into God's presence both by setting Him before us and by setting our prayers before Him.

2. Prayer is the heart of worship.

Our prayers are received as gold before God. They are heard in Heaven in the middle of worship.

"You are worthy, our Lord and God, to receive glory and honor and power, for You created all things, and by Your will they were created and have their being."

Then I saw in the right hand of Him who sat on the throne a scroll.... . And I saw a mighty angel proclaiming in a loud voice, "Who is worthy to...open the scroll?" But no one...could open the scroll or even look inside it. ... Then one of the elders said to me, "...See, the Lion of the tribe of Judah...is able to open the scroll...."

He came and took the scroll from the right hand of Him who sat on the throne. And when He had taken it, the four living creatures and the twenty-four elders fell down before the Lamb. Each one had a harp and they were holding golden bowls full of incense, which are the prayers of the saints. And they sang a new song: "You are worthy to take the scroll and to open its seals..." (Rev. 4:11–5:9).

3. Confession prepares us for worship.

During Nehemiah's time, God's people stood for three hours studying and reading the Word of God! They spent an additional three hours in confession and worship. Today we sit in church for one hour and we are ready to leave at the end of that time.

Those of Israelite descent...stood in their places and confessed their sins and the wickedness of their fathers. They stood where they were and read from the Book of the Law of the Lord their God for a quarter of the day, and spent another quarter in confession and in worshiping the Lord their God (Neh. 9:2-3).

We see here that confession and worship go hand in hand. If we don't include confession in our prayer life, our Christian walk will be dampened, as will our worship and our relationship with God. Concealing our sins will cause us to fail to prosper in God's presence (Prov. 28:13).

Is Worship Worth Dying For?

By faith Jacob, when he was dying, blessed each of Joseph's sons, and worshiped as he leaned on the top of his staff (Heb. 11:21).

Early in Jacob's life, he entered the presence of the living God, though he did not know God was with him (Gen. 28:11-17). Now in his last days, Jacob continued to rely on his faith in this God he had met. Leaning his sick, frail body on his staff, Jacob worshiped God!

Is the privilege of worshiping God worth as much as your remaining days on earth? Think carefully about this, because worshiping God is the highest occupation you can enjoy.

Saints Who Worshiped God

- **Abraham**
  From there he went on toward the hills east of Bethel and pitched his tent, with Bethel on the west and Ai on the east. There he built an altar to the Lord and called on the name of the Lord (Gen. 12:8).

- **Abraham's Servant**
  And I bowed down and worshiped the Lord. I praised the Lord, the God of my master Abraham... (Gen. 24:48).

- **Jacob**
  By faith Jacob, when he was dying, blessed each of Joseph's sons, and worshiped as he leaned on the top of his staff (Heb. 11:21).

- **The Israelites**
  ...when they heard that the Lord was concerned about them and had seen their misery, they bowed down and worshiped (Ex. 4:31).

- **Moses**
  Moses bowed to the ground at once and worshiped (Ex. 34:8).

- **Samuel, Elkanah, and Hannah**
  Early the next morning they arose and worshiped before the Lord ... (1 Sam. 1:19).

- **Job**
  At this, Job got up and tore his robe and shaved his head. Then he fell to the ground in worship (Job 1:20).

- **David**
  ...And the king bowed in worship on his bed and said, "Praise be to the Lord, the God of Israel..." (1 Kings 1:47b-48).

- **Jehoshaphat**
  Jehoshaphat bowed with his face to the ground, and all the people of Judah and Jerusalem fell down in worship before the Lord (2 Chron. 20:18).

- **Hezekiah**
  When the offerings were finished, the king [Hezekiah] and everyone present with him knelt down and worshiped (2 Chron. 29:29).

- **Jonah**
  He [Jonah] answered, "I am a Hebrew and I worship the Lord, the God of heaven, who made the sea and the land" (Jon. 1:9).

- **Jesus' Disciples**
  Then they worship Him and returned to Jerusalem with great joy (Lk. 24:52).

- **A Blind Man**
  Then the [blind] *man said, "Lord, I believe," and he worshiped Him* (Jn. 9:38).

- **Mary and Mary Magdalene**
  Suddenly Jesus met them. "Greetings," He said. They came to Him, clasped His feet and worshiped Him (Mt. 28:9).

- **Paul**
  However, I admit that I worship the God of our fathers as a follower of the Way... (Acts 24:14).

Chapter 5

Forsake Him Not in Worship!

Part 2

Worship the Lord with gladness; come before Him with joyful songs (Ps. 100:2).

In Part 1 we examined the importance and the background of worship. Now, let us discover how to put worship into practice in everyday living. As you study this chapter, take the time to worship the Lord as you read. May your heart be encouraged to sense the importance of responding to our Master in worship. Worship is the response of Heaven to the presence of God. Continually, the heavenly beings surround God's throne with praise and adoration.

All the angels were standing around the throne and around the elders and the four living creatures. They fell down on their faces before the throne and worshiped God, saying: "Amen! Praise and glory and wisdom and thanks and honor and power and strength be to our God for ever and ever and ever. Amen!" (Rev. 7:11-12)

The eternal worship in Heaven is to be mirrored in our worship on earth. Praise and adoration must also be our daily offering to God. Praising the Lord is not a option for believers. It is imperative! If we do not practice the art of praising God, we are not walking in obedience to Him. Neither will we be prepared to join with the heavenly throngs when our days here are past. God seeks our praise!

"I tell you, " [Jesus] *replied, "if they keep quiet, the stones will cry out"* (Lk. 19:40).

Praise and Thanksgiving: The Gate Into God's Presence

God has given every believer a key to come into His presence and worship. This key is the word *enter*. Yes, we can enter into God's presence with praise and thanksgiving.

The Israelites who worshiped God at the Tabernacle approached Him through the gate with praise and into the court area with thanksgiving.

Enter His gates with thanksgiving and His courts with praise; give thanks to Him and praise His name (Ps. 100:4).

Therefore, God's people entered into His presence with thanksgiving and praise.

The Temple gate is called the gate of righteousness because only the righteous were allowed to enter. We are permitted to enter into God's presence because God has made us righteous and holy through His Son Jesus (1 Cor. 1:30). This is a spiritual entrance and the gate is a picture of the Lord Jesus Christ. Because of Him, we may enter God's presence and enjoy permanent fellowship with

Him. Jesus is the only way to the Father (Jn. 14:6); He is the door for God's sheep (Jn. 10:9). Hence, we should come to worship with an attitude of praise and thanksgiving because God has removed the barriers that separated us from His presence.

Open for me the gates of righteousness; I will enter and give thanks to the Lord. This is the gate of the Lord through which the righteous may enter (Ps. 118:19-20).

Praise and Thanksgiving Go Together

When the Temple in Jerusalem was finished and the Ark of the Covenant was about to be placed in the Most Holy Place, praise and thanksgiving filled the Temple. Musicians and singers stood at the east side of the altar and 120 priests were in attendance. As the musicians joined the singers in praise to the Lord, the glory of God filled the Temple with a cloud.

The trumpeters and singers joined in unison, as with one voice, to give praise and thanks to the Lord. Accompanied by trumpets, cymbals and other instruments, they raised their voices in praise to the Lord and sang: "He is good; His love endures forever." Then the temple of the Lord was filled with a cloud (2 Chron. 5:13).

After the Temple had been destroyed and the people under the direction of Nehemiah were preparing to rebuild it, they remembered the importance of praising and thanking God in their worship. As they gathered to dedicate the wall of Jerusalem, they sought out Levites to celebrate the dedication joyfully *"with songs of thanksgiving and with the music of cymbals, harps and lyres"* (Neh. 12:27). Singers also joined in the worship, with large choirs sharing in the giving of thanks. This service to God through the gift of music continued in the rebuilt Temple. (See Nehemiah 12:27-47.)

Songs of praise and thanksgiving should also fill our worship. They are gifts from God to be used in the celebration of His glory. But how shall we praise Him?

Praise God's Name

In Chapter 2 we affirmed the importance of knowing the various names of God. Now we lift up the need to *praise* God's name.

Sing to the Lord, you saints of His; praise His holy name (Ps. 30:4).

Let them praise Your great and awesome Name—He is holy (Ps. 99:3).

Praise be to His glorious name forever; may the whole earth be filled with His glory. Amen and Amen (Ps. 72:19; see also Ps. 97:12).

Because God's name is holy, we can sing songs that will bring praise and honor to Him both in this world and the world to come. There are no limits when, where, or how long we may praise God's name. We can praise Him from sun up till sun down. We can praise Him everyday, throughout the day. Unfortunately, many of us are guilty of not praising Him at all. When we neglect to praise God, we fail to obey Him because He commands us throughout the Scriptures to praise His magnificent name.

Praise the Lord. Praise, O servants of the Lord, praise the name of the Lord. Let the name of the Lord be praised, both now and forevermore (Ps. 113:1-2).

I will exalt You, my God the King; I will praise Your name for ever and ever. Every day I will praise You and extol Your name for ever and ever (Ps. 145:1-2).

Praise God From the Temple Within

In the Old Testament, the Temple was the dwelling place of God. Even after Jesus' ascension into Heaven, the disciples continued to go to the Temple for worship and praise.

Then they [the disciples] *worshiped Him and returned to Jerusalem with great joy. And they stayed continually at the temple, praising God* (Lk. 24:52-53).

Today, God desires that we should worship Him from within. This spiritual worship is possible because Jesus now sits at the right hand of the Father, and the Spirit He sent after He left this earth now lives in us (Jn. 14:15-18). Through the Spirit, the Father and the Son dwell within us if we are born-again believers, and we become God's temple.

Don't you know that you yourselves are God's temple and that God's Spirit lives in you? (1 Cor. 3:16)

Jesus replied, "If anyone loves Me, he will obey My teaching. My Father will love him, and We will come to him and make Our home with him (Jn. 14:23).

When or where we participate in this spiritual worship is not important. The crucial fact is whether or not we welcome God and enthrone Him in our hearts through praise and adoration. Our sanctuary of praise is within us. Unlike the disciples and all the Israelites before them, we do not have to seek a specific building to share in His praise. Praise and worship may be on our lips and in our thoughts at all times because God desires that we should worship Him from the temple within us.

Praise the Lord, O my soul; all my inmost being, praise His holy name. Praise the Lord, O my soul, and forget not all His benefits... (Ps. 103:1-2).

Remember, the holy Trinity lives and dwells in you.

An Important Lesson on Praising God

Now on His way to Jerusalem, Jesus traveled along the border between Samaria and Galilee. As He was going into a village, ten men who had leprosy met Him. They stood at a distance and called out in a loud voice, "Jesus, Master, have pity on us!"

When He saw them, He said, "Go, show yourselves to the priests." And as they went, they were cleansed. One of them, when he saw he was healed, came back, praising God in a loud voice. He threw himself at Jesus' feet and thanked Him—and he was a Samaritan.

Jesus asked, "Were not all ten cleansed? Where are the other nine? Was no one found to return and give praise to God except this foreigner?" (Lk. 17:11-18)

Here we have the story of ten lepers who cried out for our Lord to heal them of the dreaded disease of leprosy. Although leprosy is a horrible physical disease, it is also a picture of sin. All ten lepers were physically healed by Jesus. All who repent of sin and return to God through Jesus Christ are spiritually healed by the cleansing blood of Jesus.

Healing of the physical body is not always the will of God for the Christian, but spiritual healing always is. Yet this healing is not Jesus' primary concern. He looks for a spirit of thankfulness and an attitude of gratefulness. When the one leper returned, Jesus asked him what had happened to the other nine.

Are you careful to receive God's good gifts with thankfulness and gratefulness? Did you praise and thank Him when He cleansed you from your sins? Are you continually grateful for the spiritual wholeness He is working in you? Be careful not to forget all the Lord has done for you. Take a few minutes right now to praise and thank Him for His gift of salvation and His daily mercies of forgiveness.

Giving Thanks and Praise to God in Worship

When the glory of the Lord came upon the Temple, the first reaction of the Israelites was to fall on their knees with their faces to the ground in worship. With thanksgiving they proclaimed, "[God] *is good; His love endures forever*" (2 Chron. 7:3).

How often today do we see believers bowing before God in worship with an attitude of thanksgiving? God's love and goodness have not changed. Hence, we must make giving thanks to Him for who He is and what He does a regular part of our worship.

I will give You thanks in the great assembly; among throngs of people I will praise You (Ps. 35:18).

The Scriptures have much to say about our need to thank and praise God, and how and why we should do it. Let us explore its wisdom and instruction.

The Role of Thanksgiving in Worship

1. Thanksgiving glorifies and honors God.

Thanksgiving recognizes the graciousness of God and the faithfulness and the wisdom with which He meets our needs. We honor both the Father and the Son when we acknowledge Their goodness to us.

I will praise God's name in song and glorify Him with thanksgiving (Ps. 69:30).

He who sacrifices thank offerings honors Me... (Ps. 50:23).

2. Thank God for His presence.

How we should be thankful that God and Jesus are not only near us, but in us!

We give thanks to You, O God, we give thanks, for Your Name is near (Ps. 75:1a).

3. Thank God in music and song.

Music is a powerful instrument of worship that can lead us into a sense of reverence and gratitude as we approach the presence of God. When you have the joy of the Lord in your heart, you cannot help but sing and give Him thanks. Both Nehemiah and the psalmist recognized this.

At the dedication of the wall of Jerusalem, the Levites were sought out...to celebrate joyfully the dedication with songs of thanksgiving and with the music of cymbals, harps and lyres. ...I also assigned two large choirs to give thanks... (Neh. 12:27,31).

My heart leaps for joy and I will give thanks to Him in song (Ps. 28:7b).

When we believers come together, we should sing for the glory of God and thank Him for all things. This will fill our souls and hearts with heavenly joy. Do you have the joy of the Lord in your heart today? If not, begin now to cultivate it by taking your eyes off yourself and beginning to focus on Jesus with an attitude of worship.

Speak to one another with psalms, hymns and spiritual songs. Sing and make music in your heart to the Lord, always giving thanks to God the Father for everything, in the name of our Lord Jesus Christ (Eph. 5:19-20).

4. Thank God with prayer.

Whenever we pray to the Lord, we must not forget to add thanksgiving to our petitions and our requests for aid.

Do not be anxious about anything, but in everything, by prayer and petition, with thanksgiving, present your requests to God (Phil 4:6).

Devote yourselves to prayer, being watchful and thankful (Col. 4:2).

5. Thank God for His eternal Kingdom.

Let us be thankful that we belong to an eternal Kingdom that can never be destroyed by man or the devil because God is the Creator of this Kingdom. Let us be in awe of His greatness and power.

Therefore, since we are receiving a kingdom that cannot be shaken, let us be thankful, and so worship God acceptably with reverence and awe, for our "God is a consuming fire" (Heb. 12:28-29).

The Role of Praise in Worship

1. God calls us to praise Him.

God has called us to be His people so that we might praise Him in the world. We should always be praising Him for delivering us from this dark, sinful world and for permitting us to belong to His family. With the privilege of being God's child comes the responsibility to praise Him.

But you are a chosen people, a royal priesthood, a holy nation, a people belonging to God, that you may declare the praises of Him who called you out of darkness into His wonderful light (1 Pet. 2:9).

2. God alone is to be praised.

We must be careful to praise only the Father and the Son because They are the only ones worthy of our praise.

For great is the Lord and most worthy of praise; He is to be feared above all gods (1 Chron. 16:25).

For God is the King of all the earth; sing to Him a psalm of praise (Ps. 47:7).

3. Praise pleases God.

When we worship the Lord with praise and thanksgiving, and we glorify Him as God, we please Him.

I will praise God's name in song and glorify Him with thanksgiving. This will please the Lord... (Ps. 69:30-31).

4. Praise is everlasting.

Praising God is right because His Word says so. Praise will be conducted throughout all eternity.

Praise be to His glorious name forever; may the whole earth be filled with His glory. Amen and Amen (Ps. 72:19).

The fear of the Lord is the beginning of wisdom; all who follow His precepts have good understanding. To Him belongs eternal praise (Ps. 111:10).

The God and Father of the Lord Jesus, who is to be praised forever... (2 Cor. 11:31).

5. Praise is ordained by God.

Even before the foundation of the world, God ordained praise.

From the lips of children and infants You have ordained praise because of Your enemies, to silence the foe and the avenger (Ps. 8:2).

We can see that the fulfillment of this psalm took place when the children began praising Jesus as He rode into Jerusalem. Jesus welcomed their praises. Indeed, He never rejected anyone for praising Him. Yet some of us are afraid to praise Him when we are with other believers.

But when the chief priests and the teachers of the law saw the wonderful things He did and the children shouting in the temple area, "Hosanna to the Son of David," they were indignant. "Do You hear what these children are saying?" they asked Him.

"Yes," replied Jesus, "have you never read, 'From the lips of children and infants You have ordained praise'?" (Mt. 21:15-16)

6. Praise is pleasant.

One of the most pleasant things we can do as a believer is to praise God. The psalmist said this is a fitting thing to do.

Praise the Lord, for the Lord is good; sing praise to His name, for that is pleasant (Ps. 135:3).

Praise the Lord. How good it is to sing praises to our God, how pleasant and fitting to praise Him! (Ps. 147:1)

7. Praise God for the gift of Jesus.

God's gift of His Son, who came into the world to save us from our sins, is certainly a reason to praise God. Those who first saw Jesus at His birth recognized this, as did the angels who heralded His arrival.

Praise be to the Lord, the God of Israel, because He has come and has redeemed His people (Lk. 1:68).

"Today in the town of David a Savior has been born to you; He is Christ the Lord. This will be a sign to you: You will find a baby wrapped in cloths and lying in a manger." Suddenly a great company of the heavenly host appeared with the angel, praising God and saying, "Glory to God in the highest, and on earth peace to men on whom His favor rests" (Lk. 2:11-14).

8. Praise God for His majesty, greatness, and worth.

God is worthy to receive our praise. His greatness, majesty, power, and honor are beyond our comprehension. Yet, we often fail to acknowledge His inherent worth. Pause for a moment and let the following verses flood your heart and mind. Try to comprehend how great God really is. Then reverently offer Him the worship of praise.

For great is the Lord and most worthy of praise (1 Chron. 16:25a).

Praise the Lord, O my soul. O Lord my God, You are very great; You are clothed with splendor and majesty (Ps. 104:1).

I call to the Lord, who is worthy of praise... (Ps. 18:3).

In a loud voice they sang: "Worthy is the Lamb, who was slain, to receive power and wealth and wisdom and strength and honor and glory and praise!" (Rev. 5:12)

9. Praise God all the time.

There are no boundaries or time limits governing how or when we praise God. We can praise Him both now in this life and throughout eternity.

I will extol the Lord at all times; His praise will always be on my lips (Ps. 34:1).

I will praise You forever for what You have done; in Your name I will hope, for Your name is good. I will praise You in the presence of Your saints (Ps. 52:9).

I will praise You as long as I live, and in Your name I will lift up my hands (Ps. 63:4).

I will exalt You, my God the King; I will praise Your name for ever and ever (Ps. 145:1).

10. Praise God in the Church.

Praise in the midst of God's gathered people both builds up the congregation and fulfills God's will for the Church. Worship that neglects praise and thanksgiving will soon weaken the body and kill the congregation. Worship is an essential ingredient in the life of God's people.

Blessed are those who dwell in Your house; they are ever praising You (Ps. 84:4).

Let them exalt Him in the assembly of the people and praise Him in the council of the elders (Ps. 107:32).

Lift up your hands in the sanctuary and praise the Lord (Ps. 134:2).

Praise the Lord. Sing to the Lord a new song, His praise in the assembly of the saints (Ps. 149:1).

He says, "I will declare Your name to my brothers; in the presence of the congregation I will sing Your praises" (Heb. 2:12).

11. Glorify and exalt God in worship.

Let us come together to glorify and exalt the Lord because He is our God, and He is holy.

Glorify the Lord with me; let us exalt His name together (Ps. 34:3).

I will praise God's name in song and glorify Him with thanksgiving (Ps. 69:30).

Exalt the Lord our God and worship at His footstool; He is holy (Ps. 99:5).

May the God who gives endurance and encouragement give you a spirit of unity among yourselves as you follow Christ Jesus, so that with one heart and mouth you may glorify the God and Father of our Lord Jesus Christ (Rom. 15:5-6).

Those Who Seek God Will Rejoice in Him

As we seek God's face day by day, let us rejoice within our hearts knowing that He loves us and cares for us. Rejoicing in God defeats complaining, overcomes discouragement, and results in victory over life's daily trials. When we seek God with rejoicing, we fulfill His desires for our lives.

Glory in His holy name; let the hearts of those who seek the Lord rejoice (1 Chron. 16:10; *Ps. 105:3*).

...they who seek the Lord will praise Him—may your hearts live forever! (Ps. 22:26)

But may all who seek You rejoice and be glad in You; may those who love Your salvation always say, "The Lord be exalted!" (Ps. 40:16)

Now that you have seen the importance of praise and thanksgiving in worship, and their significance in your daily life, make it your business to praise and magnify Almighty God till you reach Heaven's shore. Then your voice will mix with millions of others as we gather around God's throne to exalt, magnify, and praise Him forever. May praise and thanksgiving be unto God now and forevermore!

Chapter 6

Forsake Him Not in Your Walk!

...let us walk in the light of the Lord (Is. 2:5).

To this point we have seen the importance of not forsaking God, of knowing Him, of experiencing His presence, and of worshiping Him. These are the building blocks that help us to walk a victorious Christian life. Without this knowledge and understanding, we cannot walk with God effectively. We can mature more quickly when we take this information from the Word of God and apply it to everyday life.

Walk According to God's Word

After Moses received the Ten Commandments from God, he received additional instructions and laws to guide God's people as they journeyed to the Promised Land. One such instruction was

God's command that the Israelites should walk with Him by obeying all He had given to Moses for them.

Walk in all the way that the Lord your God has commanded you, so that you may live and prosper and prolong your days in the land that you will possess (Deut. 5:33).

The psalmist promises us that God's blessings are upon us when we live and walk in holiness, according to His written Word. This holiness is perfected in us as we walk consistently day by day with God, throughout our lives.

Blessed are they whose ways are blameless, who walk according to the law of the Lord (Ps. 119:1).

Knowing that God truly loves us should motivate us to walk with Him. How, then, do we learn what pleases God? God's Word is the only source of truth by which we can and should live. David learned this.

Test me, O Lord, and try me, examine my heart and my mind; for Your love is ever before me, and I walk continually in Your truth (Ps. 26:2-3).

When you pray, ask the Lord to teach you from His Word so that you may walk in spiritual truth and in fellowship with Him.

Secondly, ask God to direct your heart toward Him and be careful to heed His promptings. Then you may, with holy fear, bring glory and honor to His name.

Teach me Your way, O Lord, and I will walk in Your truth; give me an undivided heart, that I may fear Your name (Ps. 86:11).

May He turn our hearts to Him, to walk in all His ways and to keep the commands, decrees and regulations He gave our fathers (1 Kings 8:58).

What would a friend, a coworker, or a member of your family say if he or she was asked to report on the effectiveness of your Christian life? Would he or she say that you are faithful to the Lord, walking in obedience to His Word?

It gave me great joy to have some brothers come and tell about your faithfulness to the truth and how you continue to walk in the truth (3 Jn. 3; see also 2 Jn. 4).

If yes, praise God! If not, prayerfully consider where you have failed to walk in God's truth, according to His Word.

Walk in God's Name

In Chapter 3, we studied the importance of knowing the various names of God and learned how to apply this knowledge to our daily lives. If, for example, we know God's name *Lord God of Truth* (Ps. 31:5 KJV), we can trust His Word and accept it as truth. Or we can trust the Lord to protect us and lead us through this dark, sinful world because we know that *Rock* and *Fortress* are two of His names (Ps. 31:3).

As we walk in God's name, using the various aspects of His nature that are revealed in His names, we can find help to meet all the circumstances and situations of our daily lives. Knowing God's names and walking in that knowledge brings power into our lives.

All the nations may walk in the name of their gods; we will walk in the name of the Lord our God for ever and ever (Mic. 4:5).

The Secret of Enoch and Noah

Enoch walked with God; then he was no more, because God took him away (Gen. 5:24).

This is the account of Noah. Noah was a righteous man, blameless among the people of his time, and he walked with God (Gen. 6:9).

Enoch and Noah enjoyed a close, intimate relationship with God. They lived with a constant awareness of God's presence with them. This was the secret of their power and righteousness.

The ungodly fail to walk with God. They neither seek God's presence nor listen to His counsel. Therefore, they do not enjoy the benefits of the godly. He who walks in God's way, as did Enoch and Noah, prospers "...*like a tree planted by streams of water, which yields its fruit in season and whose leaf does not wither. Whatever he does prospers. Not so the wicked! They are like chaff that the wind blows away*" (Ps. 1:3-4).

Which of us would not prefer to be solidly rooted in God like a tree rather than chaff to be blown away by the wind? Yet, when we live for ourselves and refuse to walk with God, cherishing the protection of His constant watch and surrendering our lives to His unfailing care, that is exactly what we become. Living in the presence of God is what makes life worthwhile. This was the secret of Enoch and Noah. They made God's word the authority by which they governed their lives and so brought glory to His name.

Is this true of your life? Can you say that you are rooted in Him like a tree planted by a stream? Do you bear fruit that glorifies your Maker? Beware lest the ungodly influence you to abandon your walk with God. The prophet Amos warns of this danger.

Do two walk together unless they have agreed to do so?
(Amos 3:3)

You cannot live a godly, righteous, clean life if you walk with the ungodly. Their ideals and life styles will soon taint your Christian life. Then, the knowledge that God's eyes are ever upon you will bring shame instead of comfort. Living in the presence of God was better than life itself for Enoch and Noah. May it be so also for you. Then others will testify at the end of your life: (Your name) walked with God.

God Strengthens Those Who Walk With Him

...those who hope in the Lord will renew their strength. They will soar on wings like eagles; they will run and not grow weary, they will walk and not be faint (Is. 40:31).

God gives those who walk with Him the strength and the power to live a consistently holy life. He does not expect us to please Him in our own strength, but to rely on His. Indeed, when we acknowledge our weaknesses and place our hope in God alone, we find that He begins to work for us. His strength is magnified in us when we stop trying to use our own strength and power to achieve victory.

But [God] *said to me, "My grace is sufficient for you, for My power is made perfect in weakness"* (2 Cor. 12:9a).

For...the weakness of God is stronger than man's strength (1 Cor. 1:25).

Our world is filled with Christians who are trying to please God in their own strength. Depression and spiritual burnout assail these many who are serving God in their own power. Perhaps you are one of them. God can do a special work in your life to restore your strength and renew your hope, but you must yield yourself to Him and acknowledge your weakness. Stop trying to live from your own abilities. Begin calling on God's name and trusting His word to refresh your spiritual power. God promises to meet your need. He cannot lie.

Those who wait on the Lord by faith, committing themselves to His leading and relying on His strength to meet their daily temptations and problems, find that God does not fail them. As He renews their strength, they soar like eagles before the Lord because God's people can do all things when they invite God to strengthen them (see Phil 4:13).

If you are fainting beneath your responsibilities, acknowledge your weakness today and ask God to deliver you from self-sufficiency. Begin to walk with God a little and you will find the strength and the power to walk with Him in much. He will strengthen you when you need it the most.

Learn to Walk With Jesus

When Jesus lived on the earth, He showed us how to live in perfect obedience to the Father. Those who claim to belong to Him must learn to walk with God as He did. This is the essence of the Christian life.

Whoever claims to live in Him [God] *must walk as Jesus did* (1 Jn. 2:6).

So then, just as you received Christ Jesus as Lord, continue to live [walk] *in Him* (Col. 2:6).

As new Christians, we learn to examine Jesus' life style and to pattern our lives after His. If we would grow in spiritual maturity, we can never abandon this practice of walking with Jesus by living as He did. The more we walk with Him, the more we will become rooted in Him. Jesus taught us the importance of this connection with Him.

Remain in Me, and I will remain in you. No branch can bear fruit by itself; it must remain in the vine. Neither can you bear fruit unless you remain in Me. I am the vine; you are the branches. If a man remains in Me and I in him, he will bear much fruit; apart from Me you can do nothing (Jn. 15:4-5).

The ability to walk with God in obedience is, thus, tied to our willingness to walk with Jesus. Although that path may not be easy, we will enjoy the light of His presence because Jesus is the light of life (Jn. 8:12) and God's light shines in our hearts when we follow Jesus in a life of faithful obedience (see 2 Cor. 4:6). With the psalmist, may the following prayer of desiring to walk with and follow the Lord be yours each morning.

Cause me to hear Thy lovingkindness in the morning; for in Thee do I trust: cause me to know the way wherein I should walk; for I lift up my soul unto Thee (Ps. 143:8 KJV).

Walking With God Involves Commitment

All who desire to walk with the Lord must allow Him to speak to them from His Word and to teach them how to please Him in all aspects of their lives. God directs all who seek His guidance, leading them into the paths that will accomplish His plans and purposes.

I will instruct you and teach you in the way you should go; I will counsel you and watch over you (Ps. 32:8).

This occurs as we rely on God's goodness and seek His power and wisdom to handle our everyday affairs. The Lord knows beforehand what will happen to us. How good it is when we choose to seek His guidance and to obey His directives. Then we can expect straight paths.

Trust in the Lord with all your heart and lean not on your own understanding; in all your ways acknowledge Him, and He will make your paths straight (Prov. 3:5-6).

We can also expect, the more we walk with God, commiting ourselves to seek and obey His advice and directions, that we will hear His voice telling us what to do and how to do it.

Whether you turn to the right or to the left, your ears will hear a voice behind you, saying, "This is the way; walk in it" (Is. 30:21).

How great, then, is our responsibility to thank God for this wondrous gift, for what would our lives be without His unfailing love and His never-ending concern for us? Our words of thanksgiving, coupled with lives of obedience, He will not reject.

Let the morning bring me word of Your unfailing love, for I have put my trust in You. Show me the way I should go, for to You I lift up my soul. ... Teach me to do Your will, for You are my God; may Your good Spirit lead me on level ground (Ps. 143:8,10).

The Spirit Illumines Our Way

The Holy Spirit, who lives within us, will illuminate the things of God to our hearts and minds so we can do the will of the Father. He cannot do this, however, if we fail to study and obey God's Word (see Jn. 6:63). When we are not grounded in God's Word, we may accept our feelings and emotions to be the leading and direction of God. This confuses us because we may feel one way one day and another the next.

The only sure way to follow the leading of God's Spirit is to test every directive by God's written Word. God's Spirit will never contradict God's word as it is revealed in the life of Jesus or the pages of Scripture. As we study the written Word of God and focus on the Trinity—Father, Son, and Spirit—we can be sure that the Spirit's promptings are God's will for our lives. Since the Holy Spirit lives within us, let us conform our lives to His leading.

So I say, live by the Spirit, and you will not gratify the desires of the sinful nature. For the sinful nature desires what is contrary to the Spirit... Since we live by the Spirit, let us keep in step with the Spirit (Gal. 5:16-17; 25).

Walk Worthy Before God

Christians must be careful not to sit back and do nothing for God until it is time for us to go to Heaven. God intends that we should walk worthy of Him throughout our lives. This occurs as we cultivate a growing knowledge of the wisdom and understanding of God, and as we practice what we learn. Faith and knowledge must be put into practice if they would benefit us. We cannot delight God if we fail to labor for Him and to bear fruit that is pleasing to Him.

The apostle Paul was convinced of this need to seek to live in a manner that pleases God. Repeatedly, he instructed his converts to walk worthy of the Lord and he commended them when he saw fruit in their lives that gave evidence of their godly walk.

And we pray…that you may live a life worthy of the Lord and may please Him in every way: bearing fruit in every good work, growing in the knowledge of God (Col. 1:10).

For you know that we dealt with each of you as a father deals with his own children, encouraging, comforting and urging you to live lives worthy of God, who calls you into His kingdom and glory (1 Thess. 2:11-12).

Finally, brothers, we instructed you how to live in order to please God, as in fact you are living. Now we ask you and urge you in the Lord Jesus to do this more and more (1 Thess. 4:1).

What might the apostle Paul say to you? Are you seeking to grow in the knowledge and the understanding of God, and are you living by what you learn? The privilege of inheriting God's Kingdom of light goes to those who, with great patience and endurance, joyfully *work* for the upbuilding of that Kingdom (see Col. 1:11-14). God's power is sufficient for the task. What are you doing with it?

Walk in the Light
Many times when I walked up the mountain at night to see why we weren't getting any water, I carried a lantern with me to light my

way. As I walked, I could see only one step in front of me, but that was sufficient to help me reach my destination.

The Word of God lights our path when we walk before the Lord in surrender and obedience. We may not see the entire path when we first approach it, but God promises to guide us one step at a time. His lamp is always burning, because the Holy Spirit within us provides an ample supply of oil.

Your word is a lamp to my feet and a light for my path (Ps. 119:105).

Therefore, we need never fear where our life's journeys might take us. The light of God's presence will not fail us. As we read God's Word and ask Him to teach us, and as we accept His discipline and correction, we can be assured that we will reach His intended destination.

You, O Lord, keep my lamp burning; my God turns my darkness into light (Ps. 18:28).

Blessed are those who have learned to acclaim You, who walk in the light of Your presence, O Lord (Ps. 89:15).

…God watched over me…His lamp shone upon my head and by His light I walked through darkness! (Job 29:2-3)

For these commands are a lamp, this teaching is a light, and the corrections of discipline are the way to life (Prov. 6:23).

Chapter 7

Forsake Him Not in Service!

How much more, then, will the blood of Christ, who through the eternal Spirit offered Himself unblemished to God, cleanse our consciences from acts that lead to death, so that we may serve the living God! (Heb. 9:14)

We cannot effectively serve God with power if we don't know Him, worship Him, and walk with Him. This service to God is part of our worship because the Greek word *latreuo* means "to worship or to serve, as in the service of God." Consequently, when Jesus' parents took Him to the Temple after His birth and there met a prophetess named Anna, the King James Version says that Anna *"served God with fastings and prayers"* and the New International Version testifies that she *"worshiped night and day, fasting and praying"* (Lk. 2:37). Our worship and our service are intertwined. They cannot be separated.

Jesus said to him, "Away from Me, Satan! For it is written: 'Worship the Lord your God, and serve Him only' " (Mt. 4:10).

Servants Are Called by God

The apostle Paul identified himself as *"Paul, a servant of Christ Jesus, called to be an apostle and set apart for the gospel of God"* (Rom. 1:1). He knew himself to be a slave of God, a position he voluntarily accepted. James, Peter, and Jude also understood their relationship to God and Christ to be that of a slave or a servant.

James, a servant of God and of the Lord Jesus Christ (Jas. 1:1a).

Simon Peter, a servant and apostle of Jesus Christ (2 Pet. 1:1a).

Jude, a servant of Jesus Christ... (Jude 1:1).

The highest privilege on earth is be a *servant of God*. There is no other title with so much honor. We represent the Almighty God as His servants. Even though Jesus gave His life for us, He will never force us to become His slaves. We must choose to serve Him.

Paul was called and commissioned by God, not by any man or agency.

Paul, an apostle—sent not from men nor by man, but by Jesus Christ and God the Father, who raised Him from the dead (Gal. 1:1).

You, too, must be assured that your commission to serve God does not come from your church or through the efforts of man. Today we see some ministries that are developed by the efforts of man, not God. Some people *call themselves* to a certain ministry. If you create a call to a ministry, you and others will suffer because God will not be with you in the work. Make sure whatever you do for God is under His commission and His direction. Only then will you truly be Christ's servant, because a servant is one who carries out his master's wishes.

Becoming a servant of the gospel is a gift of God's grace. It cannot be earned by one's own merit. The secret behind Paul's success in carrying the gospel to the Gentiles was his commission from God. God's power goes with His servants when they follow His directives.

I became a servant of this gospel by the gift of God's grace given me through the working of His power (Eph. 3:7).

When Jesus set you free from the bondage of sin and gave you a clear conscience, you became a servant of the living God.

But now that you have been set free from sin and have become slaves to God, the benefit you reap leads to holiness, and the result is eternal life (Rom. 6:22).

Serve in God's Name

Whatever you say or do as your vocation in life, do it in the name of the Lord with an attitude of thanksgiving to the Father through His Son Jesus, because you acted as a servant on Their behalf. Then you will bring glory to God, which is your purpose.

And whatever you do, whether in word or deed, do it all in the name of the Lord Jesus, giving thanks to God the Father through Him (Col. 3:17).

Follow the Master

A servant follows in his master's footsteps. Thus, anyone who wants to serve the Lord must know Him and walk with Him to learn what He does. Knowing, worshiping, and walking with God, therefore, prepare you to be His servant, a servant who is constantly in the

Lord's presence. The Father will honor you for your service to Him because you carry out His will.

Whoever serves Me must follow Me; and where I am, My servant also will be. My Father will honor the one who serves Me (Jn. 12:26).

Give your all, gladly accepting any task God gives you, and He will bless you. Any service done to please God, not man, gains His favor.

Obey [your masters] *not only to win their favor when their eye is on you, but like slaves of Christ, doing the will of God from your heart. Serve wholeheartedly, as if you were serving the Lord, not men* (Eph. 6:6-7).

I can remember the early stages of my Christian service when I did things to please other people. I was always worried about what others thought of me. This proved to be disastrous because it led to spiritual burnout. During that time, I learned that serving God in my own strength and power ends in failure.

God did not create us to be failures. He created us to succeed and to enjoy discovering what we can do by His power.

For You make me glad by Your deeds, O Lord; I sing for joy at the works of Your hands (Ps. 92:4).

Serve the Lord with gladness... (Ps. 100:2 KJV).

There comes a time in every Christian's life when he must decide whether he will surrender his will to God and serve Him without reserve. In that day, he must decide if he can serve God wholeheartedly or if serving God is undesirable.

But if serving the Lord seems undesirable to you, then choose for yourselves this day whom you will serve, whether the gods your forefathers served beyond the River, or the gods of the Amorites, in whose land you are living. But as for me and my household, we will serve the Lord (Josh. 24:15).

Perhaps you have already encountered this moment of decision. If not, or if at that moment you chose to worship other gods, I encourage you today to resolve, "As for me and my family we will serve the Lord."

Don't Depend on Man for God's Work

Many Christians who chose to serve God mistakenly look to men for their reward. Consequently, they set themselves up for disappointment because Christian service may not bring visible rewards. You will be rewarded by the Lord for your work as His servant.

Whatever you do, work at it with all your heart, as working for the Lord, not for men, since you know that you will receive an inheritance from the Lord as a reward. It is the Lord Christ you are serving (Col. 3:23-24).

There is spiritual danger in putting your trust and confidence in man to carry out God's plan. This is turning away from God because your trust is not in Him. Then you will feel like you are in the middle of a hot, dry desert with little hope for relief. You cannot prosper spiritually if you trust in man to reward or complete your service to God. Trust in the name of the Lord to accomplish His plan.

This is what the Lord says: "Cursed is the one who trusts in man, who depends on flesh for his strength and whose heart turns away from the Lord. He will be like a bush in the wastelands; he will not see prosperity when it comes. He will dwell in the parched places of the desert, in a salt land where no one lives (Jer. 17:5-6).

Some trust in chariots and some in horses, but we trust in the name of the Lord our God (Ps. 20:7).

If you are trying to do God's will to please men and to win their approval, be careful. You may find that you lose your part in God's work because you are not being an effective servant. The servant must always seek to please the master, not another servant. Examine your heart today to see whose approval you are seeking.

Am I now trying to win the approval of men, or of God? Or am I trying to please men? If I were still trying to please men, I would not be a servant of Christ (Gal. 1:10).

Servants Are Faithful

Jesus teaches us, in the Gospel of Matthew, the importance of being a faithful servant. First, He warns us to work diligently at all times because we don't know when He will return. Then we will be found faithful when He comes (see Mt. 24:42-51). Second, He tells the stories of maidens in a wedding party and servants who are given talents to invest for the master. Both stories teach the importance of being prepared and of serving well. Such service is rewarded. Those who are faithful in their service are given additional opportunities to serve, but the unfaithful lose even the little responsibility they originally had.

Who then is the faithful and wise servant, whom the master has put in charge of the servants in his household to give them their food at the proper time? It will be good for that servant whose master finds him doing so when he returns (Mt. 24:45-46).

His master replied, "Well done, good and faithful servant! You have been faithful with a few things; I will put you in charge of many things. Come and share your master's happiness!" (Mt. 25:21)

Whatever God gives you to do, do it faithfully. When you become faithful in the little things you do for God, He will reward you with greater responsibilities. God trusts you to accomplish everything that He asks of you. You must prove yourself worthy of that trust.

Now it is required that those who have been given a trust must prove faithful (1 Cor. 4:2).

The apostle Paul was entrusted with the task of carrying the gospel to the Gentile world. This was God's will for his life. Paul encouraged the same faithfulness to God-given tasks in those with whom he shared the gospel. Many of his converts also proved to be faithful servants of Jesus Christ. Thus, Paul addressed his letter to the Ephesians, "*Paul, an apostle of Christ Jesus by the will of God, to the saints in Ephesus, the faithful in Christ Jesus*" (Eph. 1:1).

How might the apostle Paul address a letter to you and your congregation? Are you faithful in the ministry of the gospel? Do you thank God for the privilege of serving Him and for the strength and ability He gives you to carry out His work? Do you acknowledge that even your faithful service is a gift of His grace?

You, with the apostle Paul, do well to thank God both for your calling to serve Him and His trust in your faithfulness. Remember, everything you have and everything God asks you to do are expressions of His love, because God gives to His people so we can use His gifts. In essence, service passes on what we have received from God. You cannot master the art of being a servant, but you can trust God's power and ability to *make* you His servant.

I thank Christ Jesus our Lord, who has given me strength, that He considered me faithful, appointing me to His service (1 Tim. 1:12).

Not to us, O Lord, not to us but to Your name be the glory, because of Your love and faithfulness (Ps. 115:1).

Moses also served God faithfully. When God called him, however, he was certain that he was inadequate to do what God asked him to do. In time, Moses recognized that he could accomplish all that God required of him because God Himself was doing the work through him.

Moses was faithful as a servant in all God's house, testifying to what would be said in the future (Heb. 3:5).

Be faithful to God and He will release His power in and through you. Refuse to be defeated or to let suffering for Christ stop you from serving Him. Even if you are put into prison or you face death for your faith, press on and continue to be faithful. Put your work for God into eternal perspective, seeing that God's reward is much greater than even your life. It is the gift of eternal life in fellowship with Him.

So then, those who suffer according to God's will should commit themselves to their faithful Creator and continue to do good (1 Pet. 4:19).

Do not be afraid of what you are about to suffer. I tell you, the devil will put some of you in prison to test you, and you will suffer persecution for ten days. Be faithful, even to the point of death, and I will give you the crown of life (Rev. 2:10).

This calls for patient endurance on the part of the saints who obey God's commandments and remain faithful to Jesus. Then I [John] heard a voice from heaven say, "Write: Blessed are the dead who die in the Lord from now on." "Yes," says the Spirit, "they will rest from their labor, for their deeds will follow them" (Rev. 14:12-13).

Joshua was also a successful servant of God. In his old age, he summoned all Israel and instructed them to fear the Lord, to serve only Him, to be faithful to God, to serve Him with their whole hearts, and to remember all that God had done for them. He recognized these to be the keys to effective service.

Now fear the Lord and serve Him with all faithfulness. Throw away the gods your forefathers worshiped beyond the River and in Egypt, and serve the Lord (Josh. 24:14).

The prophet Samuel also taught the importance of serving God faithfully with a whole heart. When he anointed Saul to be king, he warned the Israelites,

But be sure to fear the Lord and serve Him faithfully with all your heart; consider what great things He has done for you (1 Sam. 12:24).

Faithfulness, in essence, is obeying God's commandments and following His directives for our lives. We cannot disobey God and still be effective in His service. Faithfulness also recognizes that our service to God is a response to His faithfulness. We serve Him because He loves us, He is faithful to us, He fulfills all His promises, and He invites us to be part of His everlasting Kingdom.

You have laid down precepts that are to be fully obeyed. Oh, that my ways were steadfast in obeying Your decrees! Then I would not be put to shame when I consider all Your commands. ... Your laws endure to this day, for all things serve You. ... My heart is set on keeping Your decrees to the very end (Ps. 119:4-6,91,112).

Your kingdom is an everlasting kingdom, and Your dominion endures through all generations. The Lord is faithful to all His promises and loving toward all He has made (Ps. 145:13).

God Will Equip You for the Work

When you commit your will to God, He equips you to complete the work He gives you. This pleases Him and brings glory and honor to Him. If then, you are considering whether something is God's will for your life, one important test you can use is whether or not the task can be done as service to God that honors Him and brings glory to His name. If the task is from God, you will receive the resources to complete the task in a manner that is pleasing to Him, and God will receive the honor for your work.

> *May the God of peace…equip you with everything good for doing His will, and may He work in us what is pleasing to Him, through Jesus Christ, to whom be glory for ever and ever. Amen* (Heb. 13:20-21).

This equipping for service includes encouragement, hope, and strength to do and say what God requires.

> *May our Lord Jesus Christ Himself and God our Father, who loved us and by His grace gave us eternal encouragement and good hope, encourage your hearts and strengthen you in every good deed and word* (2 Thess. 2:16-17).

> *Never be lacking in zeal, but keep your spiritual fervor, serving the Lord* (Rom. 12:11).

God Gives the Strength for Service

Fear and discouragement are two enemies that defeat many Christians. Fear hinders God's work in our lives when we suspect that a particular task is beyond our abilities or we doubt whether God can truly use us. Fear also prompts us to doubt whether God can and will work in our lives for good. Discouragement blocks God's ability to use us when we get impatient to see results from our efforts or we discover that the task is more difficult than we had expected and begin doubting whether the work is only of our choosing and not from God. Then we must apply David's words to his son Solomon to our lives.

…Be strong and courageous, and do the work. Do not be afraid or discouraged, for the Lord God, my God, is with you. He will not fail you or forsake you until all the work…is finished (1 Chron. 28:20).

We forfeit much when we underestimate the value of perseverance and quit before the task is completed. God's plans do not change; our willingness to complete them does. Refuse to allow fear and discouragement to cause you to doubt the will of God for your life and keep working until the job is done. God will never forsake you in the middle of His work. He will be with you till the task is completed, and He will reward you for your service. The apostle Paul understood the certainty of this truth.

In all my prayers for all of you, I always pray with joy because of your partnership in the gospel from the first day until now, being confident of this, that He who began a good work in you will carry it on to completion until the day of Christ Jesus (Phil. 1:4-6).

Now to Him who is able to do immeasurably more than all we ask or imagine, according to His power that is at work within us, to Him be glory in the church and in Christ Jesus throughout all generations, for ever and ever! Amen (Eph. 3:20-21).

Fear, doubt, and discouragement have no place in the lives of those who are confident that God loves them and is working for their good and His own glory. This confidence permits them to speak as though God is speaking and to do far more than their human frailties would allow. Indeed, great and mighty things are accomplished for God when we serve Him with the strength He provides, giving Jesus the praise and glory for any thanks or rewards we may receive. Then we become the very hands and feet of the One we serve.

If anyone speaks, he should do it as one speaking the very words of God. If anyone serves, he should do it with the strength God provides, so that in all things God may be praised through Jesus Christ. To Him be the glory and the power for ever and ever. Amen (1 Pet. 4:11).

God Nourishes Those Who Commit Themselves to Him

In Hebrew, the word *commit* means "to roll." Thus to commit ourselves to God is to roll our lives' cares and burdens upon the Lord, trusting Him completely for guidance and direction, and commitment speaks of yielding to the ways and the purposes of God instead of seeking our own. Success is the reward of those who commit both themselves and their plans to God and who remain in fellowship with Him. We cannot accomplish any ministry without Jesus.

Commit to the Lord whatever you do, and your plans will succeed (Prov. 16:3).

I am the vine; you are the branches. If a man remains in Me and I in him, he will bear much fruit; apart from Me you can do nothing (Jn. 15:5).

When we start depending on our own strength to carry out God's work, our efforts benefit no one. Even as grapes lose their flavor and begin to shrivel up after they are removed from the vine, so God's strength cannot flow through us to make our lives pleasing to Him and helpful to others if we remove ourselves from Him.

Jesus is the vine and we are the branches. The strength and power to do a lasting work for God come from the Vine. If we cut the power between Jesus and ourselves, we will wither spiritually like a grape severed from the vine, which dries up. We must be careful to remain attached to our spiritual power by loving God and obeying all His commandments. Then He nourishes us to serve the world.

> *But be very careful to keep the commandment and the law that Moses the servant of the Lord gave you: to love the Lord your God, to walk in all His ways, to obey His commands, to hold fast to Him and to serve Him with all your heart and all your soul* (Josh. 22:5).

Let us remind ourselves each day to keep God's Word, to love Him, to walk with Him, and to serve Him with our whole heart and soul.

Servants Praise God

Servants of God have the responsibility to serve the Lord with an attitude of joy, thanksgiving, and praise. This should be our continual response for the privilege of sharing in God's work in the world. The following verses affirm the importance of this work of praise.

> *Praise the Lord, all His heavenly hosts, you His servants who do His will* (Ps. 103:21).

> *Praise the Lord, all you servants of the Lord who minister by night in the house of the Lord* (Ps. 134:1).

> *Praise the Lord. Praise the name of the Lord; praise Him, you servants of the Lord* (Ps. 135:1).

> *Then a voice came from the throne, saying: "Praise our God, all you His servants, you who fear Him, both small and great!"* (Rev. 19:5)

Serve Others

Our service to the Lord is expressed through our service to others. As we meet the needs of those we encounter in our daily lives, we please the Lord and bring glory to Him. This service may include both the doing of goods deeds and the supporting of one another through expressions of love and encouragement.

So in everything, do to others what you would have them do to you, for this sums up the Law and the Prophets (Mt. 7:12).

And let us consider how we may spur one another on toward love and good deeds (Heb. 10:24).

Gentleness and carefulness to neither cause nor take offense are necessary ingredients of our service, as are helping one another to understand the Word of God and preserving our hearts from jealousy and resentfulness. We should not create arguments, but rather show love to our brothers and sisters in the Lord and respect for all people we meet.

And the Lord's servant must not quarrel; instead, he must be kind to everyone, able to teach, not resentful (2 Tim. 2:24).

Submit to one another out of reverence for Christ (Eph. 5:21).

I can recall many times in my service for God when it was easy for me to resent the words and actions of other believers because I did not approve of the way they did things. I became defeated and miserable because I was not treating them with respect and tolerance. God has taught me not to have a negative attitude toward other workers in His Kingdom. Such attitudes cause the resentful one to fall and others to stumble. Their work can then bring no glory to God. All servants of God do well to heed the admonishment of the apostle Paul.

Do everything without complaining or arguing (Phil 2:14).

Ambassadors of the King

We are ambassadors for Jesus Christ, His representatives in this world. What an honor! We have a message for all people from the King.

We are therefore Christ's ambassadors, as though God were making His appeal through us. We implore you on Christ's behalf: Be reconciled to God (2 Cor. 5:20).

It is very important, then, that our service be pleasing to Him and effective for His purposes. Too often, however, I fear that Christians refuse to accept this title and responsibility. Therefore, as we close this chapter, I invite you to humbly kneel before the Lord and present yourself to be used as His representative in this world. Confess to Him the fear and discouragement that hinder His work in your life. Affirm your faith that He can and will do great and mighty things through you so that others may find salvation in Jesus Christ. Lay your plans at His feet and seek His plans for your life so that the name of Jesus may be glorified and you may be a pleasing sacrifice offered up to the Father. Remember, you serve the King of kings and Lord of lords who was once a servant. The following prayer may help you to come into God's presence and to offer yourself as His servant/ambassador.

Lord, here I am. I am yours. Accept me, prepare me, teach me, use me according to Your will so that I may bring praise and glory to Your holy name. "O Lord, truly I am Your servant; I am Your servant..." (Ps. 116:16).

Chapter 8

Forsake Him Not in Times of Trouble!

God is our refuge and strength, an ever-present help in trouble (Ps. 46:1).

Our world, as we see it today, is in total darkness. War threatens millions throughout the world, crime has reached a new peak, and the economy is leveling our country. Churches are not exempt from this gloominess. Many congregations are suffering the ravages brought on by unfaithful and dissatisfied members. In this final chapter, let us examine how we can handle these many problems in a complex world.

I have placed this chapter at the end of the book because it is only as we know God, worship Him, and learn to walk with Him and serve Him on a daily basis that we can triumphantly face the problems and crises that confront us. Victory belongs to those who find in God their refuge and strength.

Are You at the End of the Road?

Many times when we face life's crises, it feels as though we come to the end of the road with no detours, no new roads, and no one to stop and help us. This place often confines us in pain, loneliness, suffering, sorrow, and defeat. Many Christians today experience this heartache without knowing where to find help. Some depend on their friends or loved ones to lighten their burden, but others have no friends or family to help them. What then can they do?

The Word of God tells us that those who come to the end of the road and cry out to the Lord for help will be delivered.

They reeled and staggered like drunken men; they were at their wits' end. Then they cried out to the Lord in their trouble, and He brought them out of their distress (Ps. 107:27-28).

If we are not delivered, it is because we never ask God for help! This appears to be so simple, yet the majority of Christians today do not have the complete confidence that God can deliver them no matter what trials and circumstances they are experiencing. The lack is not in God's power to save, but in our unwillingness to seek His salvation.

God wants to help us in times of need. The Scriptures are filled with stories of those who experienced His aid. Their experience can be ours if we will but take God at His word and seek His deliverance.

God Sees and Understands Our Pain

God's people, the Israelites, were in bondage to Pharaoh and the Egyptian taskmasters. They knew nothing but pain and sorrow day after day. In their misery, they cried out to God for deliverance and

God heard their prayers. (See Exodus chapters one and two.) He saw the pain and suffering of His people and was concerned for them.

The Lord said, "I have indeed seen the misery of My people in Egypt. I have heard them crying out because of their slave drivers, and I am concerned about their suffering (Ex. 3:7).

When the Israelites heard that God was concerned for them, they bowed down and worshiped Him! Now, instead of seeing only their pain and sorrow, they looked to God.

Moses and Aaron brought together all the elders of the Israelites, and Aaron told them everything the Lord had said to Moses. He also performed the signs before the people, and they believed. And when they heard that the Lord was concerned about them and had seen their misery, they bowed down and worshiped (Ex. 4:29-31).

God knows the secret sorrows you carry in your heart even as He understood the plight of His people in Egypt. He hears your cry and wants to help you, but He will not force His way into your life.

Have you sought His help? Can you honestly say that you know God is aware of your crisis and you believe He will meet your needs? This is the beginning of deliverance. Joy begins to lighten our loads when we affirm that God knows and sees our problems, because then we are no longer alone.

I will be glad and rejoice in Your love, for You saw my affliction and knew the anguish of my soul (Ps. 31:7).

Unfortunately, we sometimes have mental blocks that prevent us from believing that God knows and cares what we are facing. We may even wonder if He remembers our existence. God has not moved in those difficult times, we have. He will not hide His face from us when conflicts and trials threaten to overcome us. He sees our situations and hears even our faintest pleas for help.

For He has not despised or disdained the suffering of the afflicted one; He has not hidden His face from him but has listened to his cry for help (Ps. 22:24).

Remember whenever you are faced with a situation or circumstance that you can't handle to ask the Lord in prayer to take notice of your need. Beseech Him to hear the cries of your heart. Then give thanks and be glad that He knows your problems and seeks to comfort you in the midst of your sorrows.

Look upon my affliction and my distress and take away all my sins. … Guard my life and rescue me; let me not be put to shame, for I take refuge in You (Ps. 25:18,20).

Afflictions Bring Us to the Lord

Sometimes God allows His people to experience affliction. This is difficult for us to understand. As we study the Bible, we see that many people came to a closer relationship with God through great pain and severe afflictions. King David and the apostle Paul are good examples of this. Both suffered much at the hands of others. Their experiences taught them to seek to understand God's plans and purposes and to trust Him in all circumstances. Likewise, the Israelites endured great calamity as God brought them into a position of humility before Him, and the psalmist found in affliction the motivation to study God's law.

But You are a shield around me, O Lord; You bestow glory on me and lift up my head. To the Lord I cry aloud, and He answers me from His holy hill. I lie down and sleep; I wake again, because the Lord sustains me. I will not fear the tens of thousands drawn up against me on every side (Ps. 3:3-6).

...I [Paul] *have learned to be content whatever the circumstances. I know what it is to be in need, and I know what it is to have plenty. I have learned the secret of being content in any and every situation...* (Phil. 4:11-12).

Then their numbers decreased, and they were humbled by oppression, calamity and sorrow (Ps. 107:39).

It was good for me to be afflicted so that I might learn Your decrees (Ps. 119:71).

God may allow different things to come into your life if you drift away from Him and He needs to call you back to His side. Unconfessed sin is often another reason He permits sorrow and suffering to afflict you. Don't complain when God allows hard times to befall you, but rather confess with Job, *"Blessed is the man whom God corrects; so do not despise the discipline of the Almighty"* (Job 5:17).

Not all suffering is for the purpose of bringing us closer to God. Some godly Christians who live righteously before the Lord still suffer greatly. Multiple sorrows or extended illnesses plague them. We cannot understand why God allows these things to happen. His ways are not our ways, neither are His thoughts like our thoughts (see Is. 55:8). Still we can affirm that God's eyes are on them and He will use their experiences for good (see Rom.8:28)—although those who suffer may not see this good.

Even then we can rejoice, because our suffering is never wasted. God's love for us is too great to allow that to happen.

...we also rejoice in our sufferings, because we know that suffering produces perseverance; perseverance, character; and character, hope. And hope does not disappoint us, because God has poured out His love into our hearts by the Holy Spirit, whom He has given us (Rom. 5:3-5).

Let us consider it a joy when God allows His testings to come into our lives. In those times our faith is strengthened and we have the opportunity to stand before Him with praise, not complaining. In so doing, we will find that He uses our trials to refine us and to produce within us pure gold that is more valuable than anything this world offers. Then He is glorified in us.

Consider it pure joy, my brothers, whenever you face trials of many kinds, because you know that the testing of your faith develops perseverance. Perseverance must finish its work so that you may be mature and complete, not lacking anything (Jas. 1:2-4).

In this you greatly rejoice, though now for a little while you may have had to suffer grief in all kinds of trials. These have come so that your faith—of greater worth than gold, which perishes even though refined by fire—may be proved genuine and may result in praise, glory and honor when Jesus Christ is revealed (1 Pet. 1:6-7).

Many believers have been brought back to God as chosen vessels because they have refused to allow the furnace of affliction to defeat them.

See, I have refined you, though not as silver; I have tested you in the furnace of affliction (Is. 48:10).

May this also be your experience. As you pass through the fiery furnace, may you pass the test of faith, being careful not to allow the heat of God's testing to defeat you. Like the apostle Paul, trust God to use your weaknesses and to transform you by His power. You will not be disappointed.

Three times I pleaded with the Lord to take it [Paul's thorn in the flesh] *away from me. But He said to me, "My grace is sufficient for you, for My power is made perfect in weakness." Therefore I will boast all the more gladly about my weaknesses, so that Christ's power may rest on me. That is why, for Christ's sake, I delight in weaknesses, in insults, in hardships, in persecutions, in difficulties. For when I am weak, then I am strong* (2 Cor. 12:8-10).

Your Midnight Crisis

Many people find their difficulties the hardest to face in the middle of the night. Darkness surrounds them and loneliness sets in. The apostle Paul and Silas, his companion, are inspiring examples of weathering crises at midnight.

Paul and Silas were thrown into prison after casting a spirit out of a slave girl and, thus, depriving her owners of the income they had made through her fortune-telling. As they sat in the prison with their feet chained and their bodies throbbing from the wounds inflicted by flogging, a miracle took place—a miracle occasioned by their prayer and song service in the middle of the night.

After they had been severely flogged, they were thrown into prison, and the jailer was commanded to guard them carefully. Upon receiving such orders, he put them in the inner cell and fastened their feet in the stocks. About midnight Paul and Silas were praying and singing hymns to God, and the other prisoners were listening to them. Suddenly there was such a violent earthquake that the foundations of the prison were shaken. At once all the prison doors flew open, and everybody's chains came loose (Acts 16:23-26).

Notice, Paul and Silas didn't complain or gripe about their awful situation. They were powerless to change that. They did the one thing they had the power to do. They prayed and sang hymns to God.

Perhaps you feel like you are bound by circumstances in life over which you have no control. You can handle your problems the way Paul and Silas managed theirs. Pray and ask the Lord to set you free from your prison. Instead of laying in bed at night and pondering over the difficulties you face, think of the Lord's presence and His strength for your life. Praise Him for those times in the past when He delivered you and refuse to complain about your present circumstances.

Set me free from my prison, that I may praise Your name (Ps. 142:7a).

Picture the darkness you are enduring as the shadow of God's wings over you and remember that even in the midst of your darkness His presence is your light. So turn your night into day and your midnight crisis into God's shadow over your life.

Though I have fallen, I will rise. Though I sit in darkness, the Lord will be my light (Mic. 7:8b).

On my bed I remember You; I think of You through the watches of the night. Because You are my help, I sing in the shadow of Your wings (Ps. 63:6-7).

God Is Our Divine Help

What a comfort it is to know that God is with us the very moment we are in trouble. The challenge in those moments is to turn our eyes without delay from our problems to His presence. This is the key. For if we fail to consciously turn our thoughts to Him and to trustingly expect Him to work on our behalf, very often we take the situation into our own hands and try to work things out in our own strength. Before we know it, the problem multiplies.

When you are in trouble, you must put your faith in God and cling to His promise that He cares for you. Use past examples of His faithfulness to provide the comfort and the support you need, and remember to praise Him for what He has done and yet will do. Say to yourself "Jesus is my helper" and place your confidence and security in Him. Then you will find the help you need to face all of life's trials and difficulties.

God is our refuge and strength, an ever-present help in trouble (Ps. 46:1).

...say with confidence, "The Lord is my helper; I will not be afraid... (Heb. 13:6).

Let us then approach the throne of grace with confidence, so that we may receive mercy and find grace to help us in our time of need (Heb. 4:16).

God promises in His Word that He will deliver the righteous out of all their troubles.

The righteous cry out, and the Lord hears them; He delivers them from all their troubles. The Lord is close to the broken-hearted and saves those who are crushed in spirit. A righteous man may have many troubles, but the Lord delivers him from them all (Ps. 34:17-19).

Notice, God delivers the righteous from *all their troubles*. We must be careful to believe God's Word at this point and not to rely on what we think or feel. This is difficult because our thoughts and feelings are often based on what we can see, while faith is based on the invisible power of God. When we call on God for deliverance, we must deliberately choose to trust Him. This frees Him to work for us because faith is the prerequisite for answered prayer (see Mt. 21:22).

When victory comes, be certain to give thanks for your deliverance and to praise God for His goodness. In so doing you please God and bring glory to His name by sharing the news of His victory with others.

O Lord, open my lips, and my mouth will declare Your praise (Ps. 51:15).

Knowing God's Name in the Midst of Trouble

In Chapter 2 we touched briefly on the importance of knowing God's name. Now we will explore how we can apply this knowledge to our lives.

When you trust and know the Lord and His name, you will experience His victory in your life. This is true because the Lord promises to protect us and to rescue us from danger because we know His name.

Those who know Your name will trust in You, for You, Lord, have never forsaken those who seek You (Ps. 9:10).

"Because he loves Me," says the Lord, "I will rescue him; I will protect him, for he acknowledges My name" (Ps. 91:14).

The King James Version translates this verse *"Because he hath set his love upon Me, therefore will I deliver him: I will set him on high, because he hath known My name."* This verse is a foundation upon which you can rest your faith. Memorize it so you can rely on it when you need to be protected or rescued. God will never forsake you, so long as you love Him and know His name. He will set you high above all the trials and difficulties that you encounter.

The Scriptures reveal that God is known by many names. Each reveals a facet of His nature and character. All can help believers through the difficult times of life.

The name of the Lord is a strong tower; the righteous run to it and are safe (Prov. 18:10).

May the Lord answer you when you are in distress; may the name of the God of Jacob protect you (Ps. 20:1).

A comprehensive list of the names of God and Jesus is available in an appendix at the end of this book. Here we will note but a few examples.

1. Counselor

We can depend on Jesus as our counselor.

And He will be called Wonderful Counselor, Mighty God, Everlasting Father, Prince of Peace (Is. 9:6b).

2. God of All Comfort

This name reveals that God shows compassion to us during our times of trouble and supports our fainting spirits.

Praise be to the God and Father of our Lord Jesus Christ, the Father of compassion and the God of all comfort, who comforts us in all our troubles, so that we can comfort those in any trouble with the comfort we ourselves have received from God (2 Cor. 1:3-4).

3. My Helper

This name of God affirms that He will help us when human strength fails or others betray us or seek to harm us.

The Lord is my helper; I will not be afraid. What can man do to me? (Heb. 13:6b)

4. My Rock, My Fortress, My Deliverer, My Refuge, My Shield, My Salvation, My Stronghold (High Tower)

This Scripture lists seven different names for God. All pertain to His promise and ability to protect us and to be the source of our security.

The Lord is my rock, my fortress and my deliverer; my God is my rock, in whom I take refuge. He is my shield and the horn of my salvation, my stronghold (Ps. 18:2).

Praise Defeats Depression

Crises often produce a spirit of depression, defeat, or sadness. Sometimes these are the evidence of spiritual burnout, as one incident breaks us after a series of difficulties. Praise is the cure for these negative spirits and the burnout that sometimes underlies them. Praise turns our eyes from ourselves and our troubles to God. It rejoices in what is right instead of all that is wrong.

If you wear a garment of praise when difficulties assail you, instead of a garment of depression, defeat, or sadness, you will find beauty instead of ashes and gladness in the place of mourning.

The Spirit of the Sovereign Lord is on me, because the Lord has anointed me to preach good news to the poor. He has sent me to bind up the brokenhearted, to proclaim freedom for the captives and release from darkness for the prisoners... to comfort all who mourn, and provide for those who grieve in Zion—to bestow on them a crown of beauty instead of ashes, the oil of gladness instead of mourning, and a garment of praise instead of a spirit of despair (Is. 61:1-3a).

I have never known a person who praises God through all things to have a negative outlook or attitude. Praise clothes our thoughts and attitudes with a positive perspective as it moves us from self-centeredness to God-centeredness. It produces a spirit of hopeful expectancy where defeat and dejection once reigned and uproots the negative thoughts and assumptions that are characteristic of depression, its enemy. Praise also transforms our outward expression from a frown to a smile. Simply saying the word *praise* requires us to turn up the corners of our mouths.

When you are experiencing heaviness or disturbance with no peace in your soul, try putting on the garment of praise. Begin to focus on God, praising Him for who He is and giving thanks for all He has done. You will find that your soul cannot remain downcast when praise is on your lips.

Why are you downcast, O my soul? Why so disturbed within me? Put your hope in God, for I will yet praise Him, my Savior and my God (Ps. 42:11 and 43:5).

Praise God in Times of Trouble

Jonah offered God a song of thanksgiving from the belly of a fish and God delivered him (see Jon. 2:7-10). Job chose to praise and worship God even after he had lost his wealth, his home, and his family (see Job 1:13-21). What a lesson for us to learn! It is not what we feel but who God is and what He has done that must govern our praise. Then we can praise Him no matter what problems we are facing or what circumstances we are enduring.

This is possible only when we know God and allow the truth behind His various names to encourage and strengthen us. His Word becomes our comfort and guide. When we have no solutions to our problems, we can blame no one but ourselves because God has a solution if we will but seek it. This solution may not be immediate or to our liking, for God may require us to go *through* the problem or difficult situation, but a solution is nonetheless available.

My soul is weary with sorrow; strengthen me according to Your word. ... Before I was afflicted I went astray, but now I obey Your word. ... You are my refuge and my shield; I have put my hope in Your word (Ps. 119:28,67,114).

Thank Him in All Circumstances

God delivered the prophet Daniel as he endured the most difficult of circumstances. When Daniel heard that King Darius, in whose land he was an exile, had passed a bill stating that everyone was to pray only to the king for a period of thirty days, he refused to obey the decree. Even though a death sentence awaited those who broke the king's edict, Daniel continued to pray to God and to give thanks for His many blessings.

Now when Daniel learned that the decree had been published, he went home to his upstairs room where the windows opened toward Jerusalem. Three times a day he got down on his knees and prayed, giving thanks to his God, just as he had done before (Dan. 6:10).

Daniel was unmoved by the life-threatening circumstances in which he found himself. Not only did he continue to pray to his God, he prayed at the window where anyone who chose to look could see him.

How unlike Daniel are we. Many times we allow the events that take place in our lives to control us instead of trusting God to control them. Thanksgiving and praise were Daniel's chosen weapons. They are also God's will for us no matter what we are facing.

Even in the midst of the most trying circumstances, God expects us to have an attitude of thanksgiving. His purpose is not that we should give thanks for the adversities themselves, but that we should turn our thoughts to Him and trust Him. Then, as we affirm that God is bigger than our problems, we open the door for God to work for us.

*Speak to one another with psalms, hymns and spiritual songs. Sing and make music in your heart to the Lord, always giving thanks to God the Father for **everything**, in the name of our Lord Jesus Christ* (Eph. 5:19-20).

Be joyful always; pray continually; give thanks in all circumstances, for this is God's will for you in Christ Jesus (1 Thess. 5:16-18).

You Will Not Be Shaken

When you set yourself in the presence of God, you are protected by His power. Those who understand this truth need never be afraid.

I have set the Lord always before me. Because He is at my right hand, I will not be shaken (Ps. 16:8).

Surely he will never be shaken; a righteous man will be remembered forever. He will have no fear of bad news; his heart is steadfast, trusting in the Lord. His heart is secure, he will have no fear; in the end he will look in triumph on his foes (Ps. 112:6-8).

You may go through problems in this life, but you are never beyond God's power and protection so long as you steadfastly trust Him. He is a fortress that nothing can penetrate. Only that which He permits can touch you.

He alone is my rock and my salvation; He is my fortress, I will never be shaken (Ps. 62:2).

We are hard pressed on every side, but not crushed; perplexed, but not in despair; persecuted, but not abandoned; struck down, but not destroyed (2 Cor. 4:8-9).

I am reminded of this protection when I hike a certain trail on the Blue Ridge Parkway. On that trail there is a huge rock where I like to sit. Many times I have thought about my security in God as I sat there in the cleft of the rock. This security is ours not only in this life but throughout eternity.

Those who trust in the Lord are like Mount Zion, which cannot be shaken but endures forever. As the mountains surround Jerusalem, so the Lord surrounds His people both now and forevermore (Ps. 125:1-2).

God's power reaches throughout all time to surround and protect His children. Only as we trust Him, can we benefit from this power. Thus, the choice lies before each of us. Will we forsake the God who loves us and continually provides for our deliverance, or will we trust Him with all that we have and are, even our very lives?

My prayer is that you will remain faithful to your calling in Christ Jesus, our Savior and Lord. May you continue to seek the Lord and have a holy thirst for the life-giving water He offers until that day when you will live forever in the presence of the Lamb who leads the redeemed to eternal springs that will never be exhausted (Rev. 7:17). Then you will thirst no more, for God Himself will be with you and He will be your God (Rev. 21:3).

Appendix

Names of Jesus[1]

Adonai-Jehovah (Sovereign Lord; Master Jehovah)—Gen. 15:2,8
Advocate—1 John 2:1
All in All—Col. 3:11
Altogether Lovely—Song of Sol. 5:16
Ancient of Days—Dan. 7:13-14
Angel of His Presence—Isa. 63:9
Apostle and High Priest—Heb. 3:1
Apostle of Our Confession—Heb. 3:1
Arm of the Lord—Isa. 51:9-10
As Rivers of Water in a Dry Place—Isa. 32:2
Author of Eternal Salvation—Heb. 5:9
Author of Our Faith—Heb. 12:2

---

1.   Used by permission of Dick Eastman, Every Home for
      Christ, P.O. Box 35950, Colorado Springs, CO 80935-3595

Balm of Gilead—Jer. 8:22
Banner of the Nations—Isa. 11:12
Beginning—Col. 1:18
Beginning of the Creation of God—Rev. 3:14
Bishop of Your Souls—1 Pet. 2:25 (KJV)
Blessed and Only Potentate—1 Tim. 6:15
Branch of Righteousness—Jer. 23:5
Branch out of His Roots—Isa. 11:1
Branch of the Lord—Isa. 4:2
Bread of God—John 6:33
Bread of Life—John 6:35
Brightness of His Glory—Heb. 1:3
Bundle of Myrrh—Song of Sol. 1:13

Captain of Our Salvation—Heb. 2:10 (KJV)
Captain of the Host of the Lord—Josh. 5:14 (KJV)
Chief Cornerstone—Ps. 118:22; 1 Pet. 2:6
Chief Shepherd—1 Pet. 5:4
Chiefest Among Ten Thousand—Song of Sol. 5:10
Chosen of God—Luke 23:35
Christ Our Life—Col. 3:4
Christ the Power of God—1 Cor. 1:24
Cluster of Henna Blooms—Song of Sol. 1:14
Commander—Isa. 55:4
Consolation of Israel—Luke 2:25
Consuming Fire—Heb. 12:29
Counselor—Isa. 9:6
Covenant to the People—Isa. 42:6
Cover from the Tempest—Isa. 32:2
Creator of All Things—Col. 1:16
Creator of the Ends of the Earth—Isa. 40:28
Crown of Glory—Isa. 28:5

Day Star—2 Pet. 1:19 (KJV)
Dayspring from on High—Luke 1:78
Deliverer—Rom. 11:26
Diadem of Beauty—Isa. 28:5
Door of the Sheep—John 10:7

Elect One—Isa. 42:1
Elect Stone—1 Pet. 2:6
Eternal Life—1 John 5:20
Eternally Blessed God—Rom. 9:5
Everlasting Father—Isa. 9:6

Faithful and True—Rev. 19:11
Faithful and True Witness—Rev. 3:14
Faithful Witness—Rev. 1:5
Father of Mercies—2 Cor. 1:3
Finisher of Our Faith—Heb. 12:2
First and the Last—Rev. 1:17
Firstborn among Many Brethren—Rom. 8:29
Firstborn from the Dead—Col. 1:18; Rev. 1:5
Firstborn over All Creation—Col. 1:15
Firstfruits of Those Who Have Fallen Asleep—1 Cor. 15:20
Flame—Isa. 10:17
Forerunner—Heb. 6:20
Foundation—Isa. 28:16
Fountain of Living Waters—Jer. 17:13-14
Friend Who Sticks Closer than a Brother—Prov. 18:24

Garden of Renown—Ezek. 34:29
Gift of God—John 4:10
Glorious Lord—Isa. 33:21 (KJV)
Glorious Throne to His Father's House—Isa. 22:23
Glory of Your People Israel—Luke 2:32
God Full of Compassion—Ps. 86:15
God Manifest in the Flesh—1 Tim. 3:16
God My Savior—Luke 1:47

God of All Comfort—2 Cor. 1:3
God of All Grace—1 Pet. 5:10
God of Glory—Acts 7:2
God of Hope—Rom. 15:13
God of Love and Peace—2 Cor. 13:11
God of My Life—Ps. 42:8
God of Patience and Comfort—Rom. 15:5
God of Peace—Rom. 15:33
God of Recompense—Jer. 51:56
God of the Whole Earth—Isa. 54:5
God of Truth—Deut. 32:4
God the Judge of All—Heb. 12:23
Good—Ps. 34:8
Good Shepherd—John 10:11
Good Teacher—Mark 10:17
Governor—Matt. 2:6 (KJV)
Grain Offering—Lev. 2:1-10
Grain of Wheat—John 12:23-24
Great High Priest—Heb. 4:14
Great King above All Gods—Ps. 95:3
Great Light—Isa. 9:2
Great Prophet—Luke 7:16
Great Shepherd of the Sheep—Heb. 13:20

Habitation of Justice—Jer. 50:7
He Who Fills All in All—Eph. 1:23
He Who Lives—Rev. 1:18
He Who Will Come—Heb. 10:36-37
Head of Every Man—1 Cor. 11:3
Head of the Body—Col. 1:18
Head Over All things—Eph. 1:22
Heir of All Things—Heb. 1:2
Help of My Countenance—Ps. 42:11
Hidden Manna—Rev. 2:17
Hiding Place from the Wind—Isa. 32:2

High and Lofty One—Isa. 57:15
Highest—Luke 1:76
His Only Begotten Son—John 3:16
Holy—Isa. 57:15
Holy and Awesome—Ps. 111:9
Holy and True—Rev. 6:10
Holy One and the Just—Acts 3:14
Holy One of Israel—Isa. 29:19; 49:7
Hope of Glory—Col. 1:27
Hope of Israel—Jer. 17:13
Hope of Their Fathers—Jer. 50:7
Horn of Salvation—Luke 1:69

I AM—John 8:58
Image of God—2 Cor. 4:4
Image of the Invisible God—Col. 1:15
Immanuel (God with Us)—Matt. 1:23

Jehovah-Elohay (The Lord My God)—Zech. 14:5
Jehovah-Eloheka (The Lord Your God)—Exod. 20:2
Jehovah-Elohim (The Eternal Creator)—Gen. 2:4-25
Jehovah-Elyon (The Lord Most High)—Ps. 7:17
Jehovah-Hosenu (The Lord Our Maker)—Ps. 95:6
Jehovah-Jireh (The Lord Will Provide)—Gen. 22:8-14
Jehovah-Mekaddishkem (The Lord Our Sanctifier)—Lev. 20:8
Jehovah-Nissi (The Lord My Banner)—Exod. 17:15
Jehovah-Rohi (The Lord My Shepherd)—Ps. 23:1
Jehovah-Ropheka (The Lord Your Healer)—Exod. 15:26
Jehovah-Sabaoth (The Lord of Hosts)—1 Sam. 1:3; Isa. 6:3
Jehovah-Shalom (The Lord Our Peace)—Judg. 6:24
Jehovah-Shammah (The Lord Is There)—Ezek. 48:35
Jehovah-Tsidkenu (The Lord Our Righteousness)—Jer. 23:6; 33:16
Jesus Christ the Righteous—1 John 2:1
Judge and Lawgiver—Isa. 33:22

Judge of the Living and the Dead—Acts 10:42
Just One—Acts 7:52

King—Zech. 14:16
King In His Beauty—Isa. 33:17
King of Glory—Ps. 24:10
King of Israel—John 1:49
King of Jacob—Isa. 41:21
King of Kings—Rev. 17:14
King of Peace—Heb. 7:2
King of Righteousness—Heb. 7:2
King of the Saints—Rev. 15:3
King over All the Earth—Zech. 14:9
King's Son—Ps. 72:1

Lamb in the Midst of the Throne—Rev. 7:17
Lamb of God—John 1:29
Lamb Slain—Rev. 5:12
Lamb without Blemish—1 Pet. 1:19
Leader—Isa. 55:4
Life-Giving Spirit—1 Cor. 15:45
Light of Israel—Isa. 10:17
Light of Men—John 1:4
Light of the City—Rev. 21:23
Light to the Gentiles—Isa. 42:6; Luke 2:32
Light of the Morning—2 Sam. 23:4
Light of the World—John 8:12
Lily of the Valleys—Song of Sol. 2:1
Lion of the Tribe of Judah—Rev. 5:5
Living Bread—John 6:51
Living Stone—1 Pet. 2:4
Lord—Rom. 10:13
Lord and Savior Jesus Christ—2 Pet. 3:18

Lord of Both the Dead and the Living—Rom. 14:9
Lord from Heaven—1 Cor. 15:47
Lord God Almighty—Rev. 4:8
Lord God of Truth—Ps. 31:5
Lord God Omnipotent—Rev. 19:6
Lord Mighty in Battle—Ps. 24:8
Lord Most High—Ps. 47:2
Lord of All—Acts 10:36
Lord of All the Earth—Zech. 6:5
Lord of Lords—Rev. 17:14
Lord Our Maker—Ps. 95:6
Lord Our Righteousness—Jer. 23:6
Lord over All—Rom. 10:12
Lord Strong and Mighty—Ps. 24:8
Lord Who Created the Heavens—Isa. 45:18
Lord Your Redeemer—Isa. 43:14
Love—1 John 4:8

Maker—Isa. 17:7
Maker of All Things—Jer. 51:19
Man Attested by God—Acts 2:22
Man of Sorrows—Isa. 53:3
Man of War—Exod. 15:3
Manna—Exod. 16:31
Master of the House—Luke 13:25
Mediator—Job 9:33; 1 Tim. 2:5
Mediator of a Better Covenant—Heb. 8:6
Mediator of the New Covenant—Heb. 12:24
Messenger of the Covenant—Mal. 3:1
Messiah—John 4:25
Mighty God—Isa. 9:6
Mighty One—Ps. 45:3
Mighty One of Israel—Isa. 30:29

Mighty One of Jacob—Isa. 60:16
Minister of the Sanctuary—Heb. 8:2
Morning Star—Rev. 2:28
Morning without Clouds—2 Sam. 23:4
Most High—Ps. 18:13
Most Holy—Dan. 9:24
My Beloved—Matt. 12:18
My Elect One—Isa. 42:1
My Fortress—Ps. 18:2
My Glory—Ps. 3:3
My Help—Ps. 115:11
My Helper—Heb. 13:6
My High Tower—Ps. 144:2
My Hope—Ps. 71:5
My Lamp—2 Sam. 22:29
My Lord and My God—John 20:28
My Maker—Job 35:10
My Portion—Pss. 73:26; 119:57
My Power— 2 Sam. 22:33
My Righteous Servant—Isa. 53:11
My Rock of Refuge—Ps. 31:2
My Salvation—Ps. 38:22
My Shepherd—Ps. 23:1
My Shield—2 Sam. 22:3
My Song—Isa. 12:2
My Strength—2 Sam. 22:3
My Strength and My Song—Isa. 12:2
My Support—2 Sam. 22:19; Ps. 18:18
My Well Beloved—Isa. 5:1

O Lord God of Hosts—Ps. 59:5
Offering—Eph. 5:2
Ointment Poured Forth—Song of Sol. 1:3

One I Love—Song of Sol. 3:2
One Shepherd—John 10:16
One Who Shall Have Dominion—Num. 24:19
Only Begotten of the Father—John 1:14
Only Wise God—1 Tim. 1:17 (KJV)
Our Hope—1 Tim. 1:1
Our Great God—Titus 2:13
Our Lawgiver—Isa. 33:22
Our Passover—1 Cor. 5:7
Our Peace—Eph. 2:14
Our Potter—Isa. 64:8

Peace Offering—Lev. 3:1-5
Physician—Luke 4:23
Polished Shaft—Isa. 49:2
Portion of Jacob—Jer. 10:16; 51:19
Portion of My Inheritance—Ps. 16:5
Precious Stone—1 Pet. 2:6
Priest Forever—Heb. 5:6
Prince and Savior—Acts 5:30-31
Prince of Life—Acts 3:15
Prince of Peace—Isa. 9:6
Prince of Princes—Dan. 8:25
Propitiation for Our Sins—1 John 2:2

Rabbi—John 1:49
Rain upon the Mown Grass—Ps. 72:6
Ransom—Mark 10:45
Redeemer—Isa. 59:20
Refiner and Purifier—Mal. 3:3
Refuge from the Storm—Isa. 25:4
Resting Place—Jer. 50:6
Restorer—Ps. 23:3

Resurrection—John 11:25
Resurrection and the Life—John 11:25
Rewarder—Heb. 11:6
Righteous Judge—2 Tim. 4:8
Rock of My Salvation—2 Sam. 22:47
Rock of Offense—1 Pet. 2:8; Isa. 8:14
Rock That Is Higher Than I—Ps. 61:2
Rod of Your Strength—Ps. 110:2
Rod from the Stem of Jesse—Isa. 11:1
Root of David—Rev. 5:5
Roof of Jesse—Isa. 11:10
Root Out of Dry Ground—Isa. 53:2
Rose of Sharon—Song of Sol. 2:1
Ruler—Micah 5:2
Ruler over the Kings of the Earth—Rev. 1:5

Sanctuary—Isa. 8:14
Savior of the World—1 John 4:14
Shade from the Heat—Isa. 25:4
Shadow of a Great Rock in a Weary Land—Isa. 32:2
Shelter for His People—Joel 3:16
Shepherd—Gen. 49:24
Shepherd of Israel—Ps. 80:1
Shield—2 Sam. 22:31
Shield of Your Help—Deut. 33:29
Shiloh (Peacemaker)—Gen. 49:10
Sign—Luke 2:34
Son—1 John 4:14
Son of God—John 1:34
Son of Mary—Mark 6:3
Son of the Father—2 John 3
Son of the Highest—Luke 1:32
Son of the Most High God—Mark 5:7

Spirit of Justice—Isa. 28:5-6
Star Out of Jacob—Num. 24:17
Stone—Matt. 21:42
Stone Cut Out without Hands—Dan. 2:34-35
Stone of Israel—Gen. 49:24
Stone of Stumbling—1 Pet. 2:8
Strength of My Life—Ps. 27:1
Strength to the Needy—Isa. 25:4
Strength to the Poor—Isa. 25:4
Strong Lord—Ps. 89:8 (KJV)
Strong Tower—Ps. 61:3
Stronghold—Nahum 1:7
Sun and Shield—Ps. 84:11
Sun of Righteousness—Mal. 4:2
Sure Foundation—Isa. 28:16
Surety—Heb. 7:22
Sword of Your Majesty—Deut. 33:29

Teacher—Matt. 23:8; John 13:13
Tender Grass—2 Sam. 23:4
Testator—Heb. 9:16
That Eternal Life—1 John 1:2
That Spiritual Rock—1 Cor. 10:4
Tower of Salvation—2 Sam. 22:51
Trap and a Snare—Isa. 8:14
Tried Stone—Isa. 28:16
True Bread from Heaven—John 6:32
True God—1 John 5:20
True Light—John 1:9

Understanding—Prov. 8:14
Unspeakable Gift—2 Cor. 9:15 (KJV)
Upholder of All Things—Heb. 1:3

Vine—John 15:5

Way, the Truth, the Life—John 14:6
Wisdom—Prov. 8:12
Wisdom of God—1 Cor. 1:24
Witness to the People—Isa. 55:4
Wonderful—Isa. 9:6
Word—John 1:1
Word of God—Rev. 19:13
Word of Life—1 John 1:1

Your Confidence—Prov. 3:26
Your Everlasting Light—Isa. 60:20
Your Exceedingly Great Reward—Gen. 15:1
Your Holy One—Acts 2:27
Your Keeper—Ps. 121:5
Your King—Zech. 9:9
Your Maker—Isa. 54:5
Your Shade—Ps. 121:5
Your Shield—Gen. 15:1

If the Lord has blessed your life by reading this book, I would love to hear from you. When you write, I will put you on our mailing list and keep you updated on any future information regarding this ministry.

WRITE TO:

Forsake Him Not! Ministries
P.O. Box 242
Black Mountain, NC 28711